Skateboarding:
New Levels

Tips and Tricks for Serious Riders

Doug Werner
Steve Badillo

Tracks Publishing
San Diego, California

Photography by
Steve Badillo
Steve Chalme
Mikey Pacheco
Doug Werner

Skateboarding: New Levels

Tips and Tricks for Serious Riders

Doug Werner / Steve Badillo

Tracks Publishing
140 Brightwood Avenue
Chula Vista, CA 91910
619-476-7125
trkspub@pacbell.net
www.startupsports.com

Copyright © 2002 by Doug Werner
Second Printing 1-2003

Publisher's Cataloging-in-Publication

Werner, Doug, 1950-
   Skateboarding : new levels : tips and tricks for
serious riders / by Doug Werner and Steve Badillo. –
1st ed.
   p. cm.
   Includes bibliographical references and index.
   LCCN: 2002105657
   ISBN: 1-884654-16-9

   1. Skateboarding.   I. Badillo, Steve.   II. Title.

GV859.8.W472 2002   796.22
                       QBI02-200386

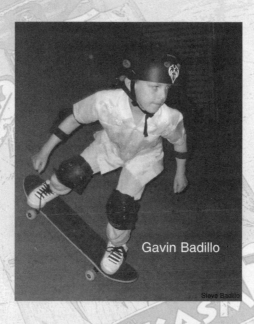

Gavin Badillo

Steve Badillo

To

the kids of skateboarding

my son Gavin

all skaters that believe they are young at heart

the sport and life we love so much

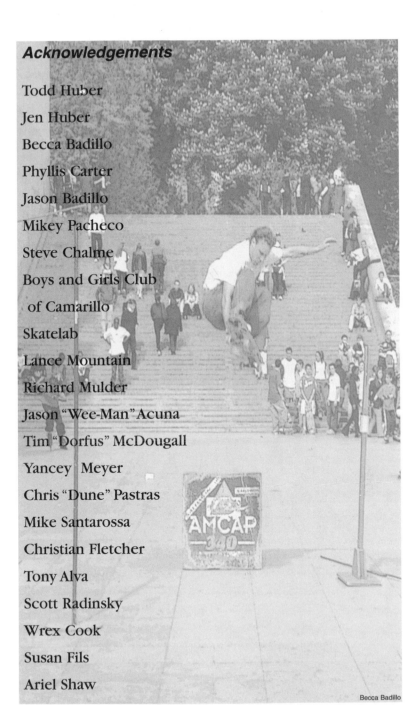

Acknowledgements

Todd Huber

Jen Huber

Becca Badillo

Phyllis Carter

Jason Badillo

Mikey Pacheco

Steve Chalme

Boys and Girls Club
 of Camarillo

Skatelab

Lance Mountain

Richard Mulder

Jason "Wee-Man" Acuna

Tim "Dorfus" McDougall

Yancey Meyer

Chris "Dune" Pastras

Mike Santarossa

Christian Fletcher

Tony Alva

Scott Radinsky

Wrex Cook

Susan Fils

Ariel Shaw

Becca Badillo

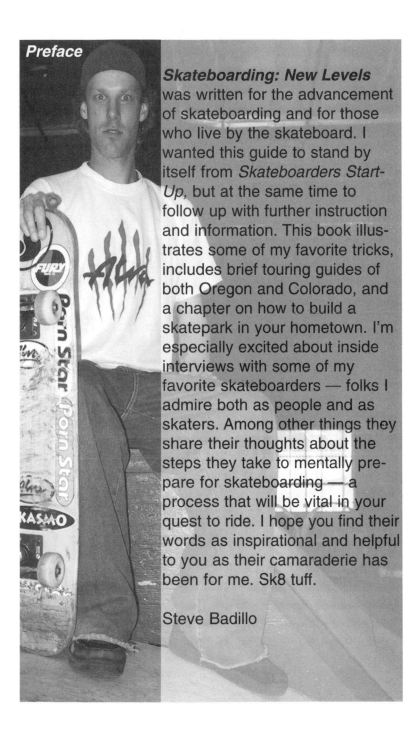

Skateboarding: New Levels was written for the advancement of skateboarding and for those who live by the skateboard. I wanted this guide to stand by itself from *Skateboarders Start-Up*, but at the same time to follow up with further instruction and information. This book illustrates some of my favorite tricks, includes brief touring guides of both Oregon and Colorado, and a chapter on how to build a skatepark in your hometown. I'm especially excited about inside interviews with some of my favorite skateboarders — folks I admire both as people and as skaters. Among other things they share their thoughts about the steps they take to mentally prepare for skateboarding — a process that will be vital in your quest to ride. I hope you find their words as inspirational and helpful to you as their camaraderie has been for me. Sk8 tuff.

Steve Badillo

Contents

Warning label
Skateboarding can be dangerous. You will fall down as you learn. Riders should know and follow safe skateboarding procedures at all times and wear appropriate safety gear.

Becca Badillo

relax

focus

commit

We talked to ten sponsored pros with over 175 years of combined skating experience including a century as professionals. In alphabetical order they are:

Susan Fils

Jason "Wee-man" Acuna
I've been skating for 15 years, 6 years pro. I'm sponsored by Dogtown Skateboards, Grind King Trucks, Epik Footwear, Shorty's Hardware, Von Zipper Eyewear, 1984 Clothing and Old Star Skateshop.

The main reason I skate is just because it's fun. I also love freeing myself from the world and doing my own individual thing.

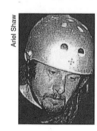

Ariel Shaw

Tony Alva
I've skated 34 years nonstop, 25 years as a professional. My sponsors are Vans, Black Flys, Fresh Jive, Rector ... I think that's it ... oh yeah, and Alva.

I like to skate pools, skateparks and a little bit of street. It's for the adrenaline rush, it's fun and keeps me healthy.

Steve Badillo

I've been skating 18 years. Tony Alva gave me my first model in 1994 so I guess I've been pro 8 years. Sponsors are Alva Skateboards, SkateLab, Porn Star Clothing, DVS Shoes, Fury Trucks and Bokasmo.

I skate because skateboarding is in me. It allows me to be creative and express my being. It fills me and leaves me feeling like I make a difference.

Christian Fletcher

I've skated since like Carlsbad Skate Park in '75. I'm 31 now. I've skated my whole life, basically. Sponsors — I don't know — all depends on the day. Omar one day, Danny Way the next — it all really depends.

It's super fun, I love to do it and I couldn't imagine my life without it. I've surfed professionally — but I have skateboarded my whole life. Actually, I try to skate on my surfboard and surf on my skateboard — kind of mix and match.

Steve Badillo

Tim McDougall

(most people know me as **Dorfus**) I've been skating since the summer of 1986. I turned pro for Porn Star in 1998. My sponsors are Porn Star Skateboards, Independent Trucks and Clothing, Etnies Shoes and Coretech Wheels. Props go out to Bokasmo who always look after me when I'm in town.

I skate for fun, excitement, adrenaline, a living, friendship, happiness, love, peace, freedom, big bowls and pool coping.

Yancey Aaron Meyer

I've been skating for about seven years. I started a little late — when I was 18. I've been pro now for about three years. I ride for T.V.S., Randoms Hardware, Ninja Bearings, Sens Shoes, Nicotine Urethane, Bokasmo and Kona Skatepark.

Lance Mountain

I started skating at age 10. Turned pro 1982. My sponsors are The Firm, Adidas, Stussy, Fury.

I skate because of the feeling it gives me, freedom, progression, the rush and friends. To see new things. experience new places, people, spots, tricks.

Richard Mulder

I'm 24 and started skating when I was 10, so I've been skating for 14 years. I've been pro for about three years now. I'm sponsored by Chocolate Skateboards, Nike, Stussy, Thunder Trucks and Diamond.

The reason I skate is simple. It's fun.

Chris Pastras

I've skated 22 years, 11 years pro. I skate for Pig Wheels and Upper Playground.

I skate for the enjoyment and challenge.

Mike Santarossa

I've skated 16 years, 10 years pro. I skate for Evos Footwear, Chapman Skateboards, Nesta Clothing and Phoenix Trucks.

I skate because it's fun.

Mikey Pacheco

skating in your mind

We included interviews with experienced pro skaters to explore issues important to serious riders. We came up with 20 questions under eight headings — mentality, risks, learning, gear, terrain, skating's current state and future, building skateparks and influences.

It is interesting to note that their insights regarding mental preparation dovetail with the same sport psychology that our culture's sport superstars rely upon so much to improve performance. These skaters do not speak scientifically and perhaps only nibble around the edges of the various theories — but their respect for the mental side of skateboarding performance is fairly healthy.

Improvement in skateboarding like all sports takes countless hours of physical practice. Doing a trick over and over again to gain expertise and muscle memory is vital. But it also takes a thinking process that involves visualizing or imagining yourself expertly performing the trick while you are preparing and even when you are away from the park or street doing something else — like lying in bed or relaxing on the couch. There's evidence that deep and detailed thinking about an athletic performance maps things out in your mind, nerves and muscles. When you actually perform, your body will naturally follow the map you created for yourself.

How you think can positively affect your emotional state and improve concentration. For example, before trying a new trick you can boost confidence, overcome fears and increase focus by first remembering how you felt the last time you successfully landed a new trick. Once your mind has taken you to that triumphant place, you can visualize the motion and mechanics of the entire trick you will be attempting to sort of set yourself up. The last thing to do is relax, maybe by taking a few deep breaths, so your body can naturally do what you trained it so hard to do.

Here's the word from some very dedicated and respected skaters. Read on.

skater's mentality

How do you deal with fear?

Acuna
I overcome by thinking of positive things. And by having a clear mind.

> The only thing you have to fear is fear itself.

Alva
You have to overcome it. Don't think about it. Just go for it. It's like they say —*The only thing you have to fear is fear itself.*

Fletcher
I get super scared pretty much. How do I deal with it? I don't know ... I just take it when it comes. I'm not sure really. Maybe it's lack of insurance. When I'm about to crash, I try to figure out something real quick to keep from getting hurt. I basically skate to skate tomorrow. Nowadays I kind of just cruise. I don't take too many serious chances.

Badillo
I try to not think about the fear so much. I know what my limits are and do just what it takes to pull it off.

McDougall (Dorfus)
I deal with fear by thinking back to the times of skateboarding that I really enjoyed (all times are, really). Sometimes I close my eyes, take a deep breath and summon a feeling that I experienced at a time when I was a young skateboarder. Then I open my eyes and hold on to the feeling I remember and go for it in a good frame of mind.

Meyer
Well, I'm very scared. I think I'm scared all the time. I usually psych myself up by pulling my hair, slapping my face, calling myself names. It sounds X-rated almost, but anything to degrade myself. I try to imagine my friends doing the same thing without hesitation.

Mountain
Not as good as I use to. It didn't matter when I was younger. You could skate the next day if you broke your arm. Now it takes so long to heal. I try to skate smarter within my means.

Mulder
If I'm going to try something that's scary, there has to be some confidence and skill in me so I can take what I call "calculated risks."

Pastras
I try to beat it by staying relaxed.

> I take what I call "calculated risks."

Santarossa
I just do. I guess I know my limits so the fear factor isn't so hard to deal with.

How do you focus?

Acuna
I focus by clearing my mind and just picturing myself going through all the motions of the trick — from rolling up to it, to being in it, to rolling away from it nice and smooth.

Alva
I try to relax and breathe deep, just kind of focus mentally

before I attempt anything physical.

Badillo
When I see the trick in my mind I tell myself that I can do it. Then I try to commit all the way.

> I focus on how good it will be after I make the trick.

McDougall (Dorfus)
I usually focus on how good it will be after I make the trick. I focus on sitting back relaxing afterward sipping a nice cold drink knowing that I earned it.

Mountain
I have to force myself to focus now, where as before it came natural to focus on skating and be clueless to people and the world around.

Mulder
Good question. I feel I need to block everything out of my mind if I'm going to skate and be focused.

Pastras
Breathing, relaxing … I clear everything out of my head.

Santarossa
Breathing seems to work best.

Do you use visualization?

Alva
Yeah, in a way I visualize the first couple of moves then I go with the flow spontaneously.

Badillo
At night before I go to sleep I think about skateboarding.
Especially when I'm trying to learn new tricks, I just think
about the steps I need to go through to pull it off. I visualize
myself in every step and then I also put together whole runs
with many tricks strung together. It is hard for me to go
right to sleep so I will be in bed thinking about skateboarding for sometimes hours before I get tired. I think
when I dream about skateboarding all the time, it helps lay
down the blueprint in my mind for my body to follow.

McDougall (Dorfus)
I don't like to visualize tricks — especially on handrails.
When I start visualizing tricks I always end up visualizing
slams.

Meyer
I usually get to a
point when I'm
trying a trick that my
mind is completely
furious and in a
frenzy. And there's a

I run through it in my mind first.

moment when I calm myself down and think about the
physics involved with the trick — foot placement, little
things. And usually when I calm myself down after all that ...
it happens.

Mountain
Your mind just does that on its own. It can see what you
need to do from watching others or trying different things.
The hard part is to get your body to commit when it wants
to sit on the couch with a bowl of ice cream instead.

Mulder
Yes, especially if I'm trying to learn a new trick. I will visualize all the motions as if I already know how to do the trick

and already have landed it and rolled away.

Sometimes I sleep and dream about doing the trick.

Pastras
Usually I visualize making any trick or line before trying it. I definitely picture myself doing each step in my head. Sometimes I just do it naturally, but most times I run through it in my mind first.

Santarossa
Yes, seeing myself land a trick in my head helps me focus and helps to alleviate the fear factor.

The basic mental trick is to just be positive.

Any other mental tricks or methods to improve your skating?

Acuna
Sometimes I go to a spot, look at it for a while and get a picture in my head of what I want to do there. Then I go and relax — even sleep and dream about doing the trick. Every time I do that, the trick works successfully.

Alva
The basic mental trick is being positive and having a positive mental attitude — that will improve your skating.

Fletcher
The way I get better on my skateboard is probably by doing other sports like surfing and snowboarding and stuff. Stuff that's similar to skateboarding but with different terrain.

McDougall (Dorfus)
You can do whatever you want with skateboarding, just open your eyes and your mind.

Meyer
I like to skate at different times of the day. It sounds ridiculous, but a lot of skaters don't skate in the morning. You may find that maybe you're sharp in the morning and didn't know it. Skating at different things at different times. Skating in the morning — go try it. It's a whole new thing. Before your cereal, try that K grind.

Skateboarding is more mental than physical.

Mountain
Watching others, skating with people a bit better and having a strong desire to be the best is the best way. To be a natural or to have the imagination to take skating to a different place or level is what makes a great skater — a skater that people will remember.

Mulder
I've come to embrace the theory that skateboarding is more mental than physical. Some say 90% confidence and 10% skill. I've come to that conclusion by being a skateboarder for 14 years. I try to keep my confidence stable so I can have a good time skating. Another method that has shown fruit in improving my skating is muscle repetition. Do a trick more than once. Better yet, do it 201 times.

Pastras
Improvisation.

Do a trick more than once. Better yet, do it 201 times.

dealing with risks

What safety gear do you wear?

Acuna
To be honest I only wear safety gear when I'm at a skatepark. I pretty much only wear a helmet.

Alva
I wear a helmet. Sometimes I wear pads underneath my pants, like knee gaskets. Depending on whether I'm hurt or not I wear extra stuff. Which sounds stupid to do it that way — that you've got to hurt yourself before you wear the gear. It's easier to skate without the gear because you're looser and carrying less weight.

Badillo
I wear really only ankle braces because I have broken and sprained my ankles so many times. Every year I roll my ankles a few times. I do wear knee pads when I'm skating backyard pools though. I wear a helmet and pads at skateparks that require them.

Fletcher
Normally, I don't wear any safety gear except when I come to skating parks. You don't really have a choice. Then I usually wear a helmet. But we've started making our own brand of pads — Think Fast Pads. I will probably be wearing them.

McDougall (Dorfus)
When I skate vert ramps I wear a helmet, big elbow pads and knee pads.

Meyer
I don't wear safety gear unless it's completely mandatory.

I've actually been trying vert a little bit more and I'm wearing some pads, but usually 99 times out of 100 there are no pads involved.

Mountain
Whatever you feel you need. You know your limits if you have skated a few years.

> # Whatever you feel you need.

Mulder
When it's required at skateparks or big ramps. Note if your confidence level is high but your skill is still beginner. To the point where you're still learning how to bail a trick safely and you're not too sure of the calculated risks, I would wear pads.

Pastras
None on the street.

Santarossa
Left knee and ankle brace. Helmet and elbow pads at the parks.

What was your worst skating accident?

Acuna
My worst skating accident was in Germany one summer. It was at an indoor skatepark with my friends. I had been skating there for a few days, but on this particular day I was doing a new trick. I was boardsliding up a railroad track rail that was on a big cement block. Well, one of the times I got on the rail too soon and locked up on my back rail (yes, I was riding rails). I flew forward and hit the block on my side. It knocked the wind out of me. Once I got back to

interviews

normal breathing, the pain in my side killed. No one saw or even believed how much pain I was in. I went to the doctor, got an X-ray and found out I had broken a rib.

My teeth cracked off.

Alva
Probably when I broke my teeth. I slammed into the back of my friend's head. We slammed into each other at the bottom of a huge bank. We almost knocked each other out and my front teeth cracked off. My friend, Les Butler, got stitches in his head. He's dead now, a casualty of our lifestyles in Dogtown.

Badillo
When I was in 9th grade I was skating with my brother and some friends when we decided to go skate behind a 7-11. To get there we had to cross the street in a crosswalk. It was evening and starting to get dark. I started to skate across the street when this car with no headlights come racing down the street and hit me on my board. I flew 70 feet and broke four bones in my left wrist, my

I flew 70 feet and broke my wrist, elbow, leg, pelvis ...

right elbow, my left leg, fractured my left pelvis, fractured the back of my head, tore my right calf muscle and lost my sense of smell. My skateboard was broken in three pieces and both trucks were bent. It sucked.

Fletcher
My worst skating accident ... I went over a spine and my board ... I ollied over the spine and my board stuck nose first on the other side and I like pole-vaulted on my taint — with a jagged tail. I just started going into shock and stuff — it was horrible — like a skateboard popsicle.

24

I pole-vaulted on my taint — with a jagged tail.

McDougall (Dorfus)
My worst accident would probably have to be from a down-hill in the dark. I mis-judged the hill and I had to jump off because it was way too gnarly.

Meyer
It's a tossup between rolling my ankle under my heavy, heavy board ... looking at the bottom of your shoe for the first time ... when you're still wearing it ... it's not a pretty sight. But I broke my nose this year, as well, and I was really scared to do anything after that for a while.

Mountain
A car crash injured my back in 1981, and there are pains I live with that make me stiff. Very sharp pains sometimes.

Mulder
Dislocating my shoulder — just for the fact that you use your arms a lot when you skate, whether you know it or not ... for balance and momentum. It's now a part of my body I need to exercise a lot and keep strong because when you dislocate your shoulder you stretch ligaments and tendons, which keep your shoulder tightly in place.

Pastras
I was knocked unconscious once.

Santarossa
Left knee, slight tear in my PCL.

How did you overcome the accident and go back to skating?

Acuna
One week later I was back at the same park skating. I was more focused on what I was doing.

> They stitched me up and sent me back out. That's how it is.

Alva
Just went back out there, man. They stitched me up and sent me back out. That's how it is.

Badillo
I had to go through rehabilitation for almost a year. My shop sponsor at the time (Aggrozone Skate Shop) was very supportive and behind me getting back on my board and doing contests. I had to almost start over with the injuries I had, but I told myself that skateboarding was all that I wanted to do. So I trained my body to get back into shape so I could get back on my board.

Fletcher
Actually, I just laid down and put some cold cans on my head for a little while and went back to the ramp (laughter).

McDougall (Dorfus)
I learned by looking at hills during the day and driving down them.

Meyer
Well, I've tried to avoid the certain trick that broke my nose. I couldn't avoid the trick that broke my ankle because it's my bread-and-butter. But the one that broke my nose, which is a frontside 5-0, I kind of avoided it for a couple of months.

Swim and Dr. G. More ice cream.

Mountain
Swim and Dr. G. More ice cream.

Mulder
Rehab. Even to this day. It's an issue that always needs to be cared for. Just by strengthening it, by muscle exercises, has given me the confidence to roach back onto my board. For me, when I get injured it's a process to get back to where I was physically — but moreover mentally. I try to take the proper steps necessary to bring me to that place where I was before an injury, physically and mentally, then past that place.

Pastras
I thought about why I slammed and forgot about it.

Santarossa
Stayed off my board for eight months, then slowly started skating again. The more I skated the more tricks I tried until I felt good again.

Visualize it and be really positive about being able to do it.

How do you prepare (mentally and physically) to do a new and possibly dangerous trick?

Alva
Like I said before, you try to visualize it and at the same time be really positive about being able to make it. A lot of times when you're doing tricks — especially the technical stuff kids do nowadays — you have to keep going over it. You must be mentally and physically persistent until you make it.

27

McDougall (Dorfus)
I make sure I'm warmed up and that I'm in a positive frame of mind.

Meyer
I try to stretch. I try to do yoga. I'm not very consistent with it, but I think it really, really helps my concentration and my flexibility when I do do it consistently. And I always ate better than most of my friends. Not too much meat, not too much sugar. I try to keep it kind of lean so I can do these things.

Mountain
You have to know in your head. Visualize it. Or just test it out low. Sometimes you just have to do it. Some of the best skaters don't think and that's why they look so good. It's not a thought-out sport.

Mulder
I ideally want to have the right amount of confidence so I can follow through with all the motions of the trick. And, of course, I will always take calculated risks.

Pastras
Visualization. Building up to it. Like doing kickflips over a curb before trying a gap. Or skating flatbars before handrails. Go small in the beginning, then bigger.

Santarossa
I never stretch as much as I should (but I'm working on that). I've always felt skating is mostly mental, so it's mostly the *I can do this!* pep talk before trying something new.

Go small in the beginning, then bigger.

learning curves

How often do you learn new tricks?

> I learn a new trick every time I go skating ...

Acuna
I try to learn a new trick every time I go out skating.

Alva
I don't learn that many, maybe one or two tricks a year, because I'm not into the technical aspect as much as others. I try to improve and polish up the things I really like to do. I try to skate with a lot of confidence, power and style. That's more important than learning tricks.

Badillo
I try to learn new tricks when I get the inspiration for it. Or I just improve on the tricks I already know and do variations of them.

Fletcher
Actually, I don't really learn new tricks. I just relearn tricks that I've already known but have actually forgotten.

McDougall (Dorfus)
With vert ramp skating, I try to learn a new trick each time I skate. Most times, I learn a trick then try to put it into a run so it becomes a usual trick. I'd say

> I try to skate with a lot of confidence, power and style. That's more important than learning new tricks.

every two sessions I make a new trick. With street skating, I do the tricks that I know but try them on and over different objects. As far as pools and skateparks, I just do whatever I can wherever I can.

> ... and I forget another trick in that same session. It's a one-in and one-out.

Meyer
Oh, I learn a new trick every time I go skateboarding. And I forget another trick in that same session. It's a one-in and one-out every time.

Mulder
I aim for one a week. If I meet my goal then I'm psyched. But that's not always the case.

Pastras
I don't usually. Or not as often as I used to. I like to improve on the tricks I already know.

Santarossa
Not often enough. It's easy to get stuck doing the same old tricks. I think my learning curves come and go. I don't try to learn a trick a day or anything. When I do learn something new, I push myself to learn different variations of the same trick. So I'll learn a bunch of things at once then I won't learn anything for a while.

Where do you get ideas for learning new tricks?

Acuna
I learn new tricks from friends telling me to try something or even by doing something by accident.

You've got to have that powerful attack to pull anything off.

Alva
Just do it. Go for it aggressively. That's usually the best way to learn anything. If you hold back or go for it half-baked, it's just going to hinder your performance. You've got to have that powerful attack to pull anything off and make it look good.

Badillo
Going out on tours and skating with my friends really helps me get ideas for new tricks.

McDougall (Dorfus)
I get ideas from vert contests because there is always new stuff being thrown down. I get ideas from skating new terrain. Some terrain forces you to learn new stuff. And from my friends and peers.

Meyer
I'd like to say the videos, but it's usually from someone you're skating with. I'll see Billy Green do a trick or Jesse Parker do a trick, and when it's your friend doing that trick, the impossibility of doing that trick is just shattered. You know someone who can do it!

Mountain
Dreams. Seeing people try things that go wrong and you can picture how it could be something else. Playing games. Having a good time.

Mulder
Lately, it's been watching old skate videos, like from the early '90s. They just

I dream them up or do them by mistake.

inspire me to go and learn a trick that has probably become somewhat extinct because not so many people are consistently doing them now.

Pastras
I dream them up or do them by mistake.

Santarossa
Friends, videos, magazines. Mostly friends. Friends push you the most.

Do you have a step-by-step way of learning new tricks?

Acuna
I go through the trick and try to figure out the best way to do it.

Badillo
I try to start out small with new tricks and when I get the hang of it, I try them on bigger obstacles.

McDougall (Dorfus)
Start off small and progress.

> The more you try the more you will learn.

Meyer
You learn the anatomy of the trick by breaking it down and making sure you can do all the components required. You can find obstacles that are similar to the one you want to attempt and just work on the setup, work on the snap, work on the speed and then take it back to the obstacle that was giving you some grief. That usually works for me.

I'm fully familiar with the motions and danger signs.

Mountain
Every trick comes different ways. Sometimes I learn low and work up. Sometimes I just picture how someone else looks or holds or turns his body. Sometimes it just happens one day even though you have tried it over and over and it seemed as if it would never come. The more you try something the more you will learn and the more probability you will get it.

Mulder
Of course, I take calculated risks. I won't try a certain trick on a huge ledge or a handrail unless I have that trick down first on an ordinary ledge or flatbar. So I'm fully familiar with all the motions and danger signs of the trick. Calculated risks.

gear

What gear do you ride? Where and why? Which board, wheels, bearings, and trucks do you ride?

Acuna

I don't have any performance gear. I wear whatever I want and skate however. I ride my signature board from Dogtown Skateboards, Ricta Wheels, Black Panther Bearings and Grind King Trucks.

Alva

I ride Independent Trucks (I wouldn't ride anything other than Independent Trucks) and an Alva board — 34 inches with a 17-inch wheelbase, nine inches wide. That's what I'm riding right now. I ride a few different shapes. I ride a 36-inch by 9-1/2-inch for downhills and banks and stuff like that. My overall board is 34 inches by nine inches wide. I ride my own (Alva) wheels. I've been experimenting with some bearings from Japan. We have special concaves with our boards like the dog-ear and triple-x concaves. I like to experiment with different concaves.

Badillo

I ride high performance DVS Shoes. I ride Alva Skateboards 8 inches by 32 inches, whatever bearings I can get, Fury Trucks from Lance Mountain (thanks) and 58 millimeter Alva Wheels.

Fletcher

It all depends really. I pretty much ride whatever I can get for free. I don't really like paying for a whole lot of skate stuff. Right now I'm riding Black Label Skateboards and Black Label Rails, but Indy (Independent) Trucks and Ricta Wheels. I ride 60s.

I don't have performance gear. I skate however.

McDougall (Dorfus)

I ride the same setup everywhere because it's big enough for vert and bowls and not too big that I can't flip it. I ride a Porn Star Dorfus Pro Model deck, which is 8-3/4 inches wide with a 15-inch wheel base, Coretech Disk Wheels, 61 millimeter, FKD Bearings and good ol' faithful Independent Trucks.

Meyer

I ride Ninja Bearings — there's no substitute for those. Ninja Bearings are the fastest I've ever dealt with. I usually like about a 56–58 millimeter wheel for my small and about 60 for pools. I like a big board — from 38 inches down to 36 and even bigger when I'm racing.

Mountain

I ride stuff I'm sponsored by or experimental stuff. I vert ride 60 millimeter wheels with a big board — 8-1/2 by 32 inches. In pools and street, I ride a board 8 inches wide because most pools are tight and a smaller wheel base turns quicker, with big wheels to go fast. On street I ride an 8-inch wide board with smaller wheels, 52 or 54 millimeter, so I can flip the board. The Firm Boards, The Firm Wheels, Ricta or Fury Trucks.

Mulder

I ride Chocolate Skateboards, Chocolate Wheels, and Thunder Trucks. I'm sponsored by those companies, but even if I wasn't, I would still ride their stuff for the simple fact that they make top quality skateboard goods. I also ride Swiss Bearings, but I am not sponsored by them. I ride them because they feel the best.

Pastras
I ride a small to medium size setup. I like lightweight setups for quick snap on the street. My boards are 7-3/4 inches wide with 55 millimeter wheels and thin trucks.

Santarossa
My setup is a 7-1/2 inch deck, 50 millimeter wheels and Phoenix 5.0 inch trucks. I ride that setup everywhere because it's the best.

terrain

What is your favorite terrain to ride and why?

Acuna
I mainly ride street but I also love riding mini-ramps, pools and skateparks.

Alva
Usually skateparks and pools are my favorite, but I ride downhills and big ditches and stuff like that, too. A little bit of street skating ... mostly bombing hills and cruising like for transportation.

Badillo
My favorite terrain would be different types of cement skateparks. I love skating skateparks with bowls, spines and transfers.

Pools ... because of the energy locked into them.

Fletcher
My favorite terrain to ride would have to be ramps and pools because it just seems more fun. I don't like getting my shins smashed and riding around the street I always seem to smash my shins and my wrists. I like carving corners.

McDougall (Dorfus)
I like to ride pools. Ones not made for skating and ones made for skating because of the energy that's locked into them. There's no opening for it to be released so it bounces off the walls back into you. I feel that there's nothing better than curved walls with vert and pool coping.

> I love skating out the door and just skating anything.

Meyer
You know, I'd have to say transitional street park. Rounded hips. If you go to Colorado, man, there's some great stuff for you to skate out there. I would say that I'd be most comfortable in a street park ... I would have to say cement. I grew up skating wood, but nowadays, the amount of cement I get to skate, I think I'm the most comfortable on cement.

Mountain
Everything. It's just skateboarding. Try new stuff and new places. But pool skating is what I grew up doing.

Mulder
I love street skating but not the drive around spot to spot mind-set of it. I love skating out the door and just ending up skating anything. That's how I grew up skating. The tricks you end up pulling are not premeditated because you end up at the most random spots. It's like a grab bag.

Pastras
Parks, mixing street with transition.

Santarossa
Skateparks. They're fun because they usually flow good. There's no hassles and they are a combo of my two favorites — street and mini-ramp.

Name the terrain that was important to your riding development.

Alva
Banks like at Paul Revere High School (in Santa Monica). That's really where I learned how to surf skate and go with

the flow. I learned a lot of footwork tricks. Basic stuff like old school balancing tricks that gave me control over my board.

Badillo
When I was real young — hills, curbs, cement banks, backyard ramps and my local schoolyards were important to my development. In the late '80s skateparks were starting to close down all over so we had to skate a lot of street. But I did get to skate Pipeline seven times before it closed down.

Fletcher
Waves were important to my riding development on my skateboard. Yeah, Trestles, Pipeline — any sort of wave helped my skating and vice versa. Like riding all the different stuff on a skateboard made it a lot better for surfing, too. Like doing airs on my skateboard. Like on a vert ramp. Learning how to do that made my airs surfing 100% better. It's kind of the same thing — when you leave the wave, the wave's vertical. Even though it's not as big, it's still the same transition type of thing. Yeah. Like the better I get on the skateboard, the better it makes me on a surfboard.

McDougall (Dorfus)
I believe learning to skate on transitions is the best way to develop skills for every other terrain. I first learned on a mini-ramp and it taught me a lot about balance, stability and board control.

Meyer
This question is interesting because where I grew up, our park featured head-high wooden hips, and I think learning how to skate on hips really helped me. I can do technical things and I can go giant! I learned everything

Balancing tricks gave me control over my board.

> **Waves helped my skating and vise versa.**

over hips before I even imagined any other way to do it. So I'd say hips had a big impact on how I skate now.

Mountain
Skateparks in the '80s. Big, open, banks, small bowls and pools.

Mulder
I grew up in Fontana, California. There was nothing but our local schoolyards, backyard ramps and homemade street obstacles — all of which were super beneficial to my progression in skateboarding.

Pastras
Skateparks. A skatepark named Cheapskates that I skated in the late '80s and early '90s taught me to skate tranny.

Santarossa
Skateparks.

How long did (or does) it take you to get comfortable with different terrains?

Acuna
When I go to a new spot, I usually warm up with the basics and get used to the spot. After that I might go home and think about the spot and think of a difficult trick to do there. Then I'll go back and do it soon after.

> **I believe learning to skate transitions is the best way.**

It's like starting over ... but it's still super fun.

Alva
About ten minutes. Depends on how good the terrain is.

Badillo
It took me awhile to get comfortable with all different types of terrains. I think empty pools were tough because they were all different and had crazy, tight transitions to learn on.

Meyer
You know, I felt pretty comfortable right away on wooden hips. Cement took me a little while to get comfortable with. I'm still a little wary of some pools. Actually most pools.

Mulder
It depends. Like vert skating — since I didn't grow up skating it, it took a lot of time and effort to become familiar with it. It's like starting over in a sense, but it's still super fun. Learning how to skate is a fun thing.

Pastras
Around six months to one year for learning transitions.

Santarossa
I started on street and my friend had a mini-ramp, so when skateparks came around I felt very comfortable. I've never been comfortable on vert because I never had access to one growing up. My main problem on vert is that I don't know how to knee slide.

from here to eternity

Where is skating today?

Acuna
Skating is more accepted and there are a lot of skateparks everywhere.

> Skating is where you want to be in your head and in your heart.

Alva
Oh man, it's like totally technical. It's big, it's crazy, it's commercial. It's this, it's that, but mostly skating today is where you want it to be in your head and in your heart. For every skater there's a different level of performance. It's where you make it.

Badillo
Skating is at a point where pros can make a living. And there are so many kids skating. Skateparks are being built all over the world and there are so many ripping little kids out there. It's very competitive. With all the skateparks, video games, skate shows and contests on TV, the base of new kids will continue to grow.

Fletcher
I think today skateboarding is headed in a better direction than it was like maybe five to six years ago or even 10 years ago. So I think now with all the parks being built and stuff, kids are actually learning how to ride transition again. They're learning how to carve corners and stuff like that. Not too long ago, kids could only ride street. You could see the best street skaters in the world who couldn't ride the simplest stuff. It was ridiculous.

McDougall (Dorfus)
Skateboarding is constantly moving and so is everything around it. Thirty years ago skateboarders were outcasts and the sport was thought to be nothing more than a fad. At the moment skateboarders are movie stars, millionaires, TV personalities, rock stars, you name it and now it's going to be an Olympic sport.

Meyer
I see skating in a weird position ... where skaters who should be recognized and should be idolized are being missed because of certain trends or certain fashions. A lot of people go unnoticed like Senn, Drehoble and Cardiel.

Mountain
It's closer to a sport then it ever was. It's looking for a few standouts with something new to bring to separate themselves from the pack. Skateboarding is accessible to so many and the learning curve so quick that most kids are quickly good enough to really have fun with it.

Mulder
Skateboarding is rad today. It will always change, but it will always be skateboarding.

Pastras
Wheaties boxes. Everywhere.

Santarossa
Everywhere.

It's closer to a sport then it ever was.

Where will skating be in five years?

Acuna

Skating is just gonna keep growing and more people are gonna be doing it. It can only go up. There will be no more downtime.

> The progression of skateboarding lies in the terrain we build for it.

Alva

In five years I'll still be skating. We'll see what happens every five or 10 years. I might say I'm just going to surf and not skate anymore. But I think I'll still be skating. I'll still be skating pools. Plus the parks are so good ... maybe I'll be down in Australia skating in Ulladulla. Who knows ...

Badillo

I hope skateboarding will continue to grow and create more opportunities for skaters to make a living at it. But for me, I want to be healthy and skating with my friends.

Fletcher

Hopefully, there will be more ramps and pools. Kids are learning how to ride transitions and stuff and then they take all that street stuff into the parks. I think it's going back to like '91.

McDougall (Dorfus)

I think the progression of skateboarding lies in the terrain that we build for it. Just take a look at Danny Way's huge air ramp. Have a look in Bob Burnquist's back yard or just go up to Oregon and Washington and feel the brutality of the concrete wonderlands that are being created by the Dreamland

Crew. It speaks for itself. If this has all happened in the last few years, just imagine what the future holds. Bring it on. The bigger the better.

Meyer
I see it taking another step toward where it was awhile ago. People going faster, people getting a little more air than they do now and not so much back and forth. You're going to see the switch stuff done really, really fast and really smooth because skating is going to be faster.

Mountain
It only gets better.

Mulder
It's up to each individual skateboarder. What they like to skate and what skateboarding is ultimately to them. One thing is for certain, which is completely obvious, skateparks are back and it looks like they're here to stay for a good while. I'm stoked. In the next few years it's going to breed.

Pastras
Still everywhere. If not, I'll still enjoy it all the same.

Santarossa
Hopefully, still everywhere.

In the next few years it's going to breed.

building a park

Have you ever been involved with building skateparks? In what way?

Make them big.

Alva
I've given input to building skateparks, but mostly guys that are building skateparks now, guys like Dave Duncan and Rick Carch, they have it down. They have certain blueprints and plans in their heads about everything they build. So I just try to give input as far as building it bigger. Make them big. I think kids should ride bigger skateparks so they don't hold back and bust out.

Badillo
I was involved with the building of SkateLab in Simi Valley. First by going to city council meetings trying to convince the city to build a skatepark, then by working at the SkateLab. I have also gone to city council meetings for Calabasses and Ventura, California.

Fletcher
I haven't been involved in building a skatepark, yet. But I have a good idea for one. I just have to figure out how to put it together.

McDougall (Dorfus)
I have recently been involved with the building of our super park in my hometown Adelaide, South Australia. The planning had been going on for years so a lot of the background work had been done. When it came time to build, a few of us worked real hard on it. We finished off the vert ramp, which clocks in at 12 feet high and 66 feet wide with a fast-as-hell top layer of steel. Next were the combi bowls, which

are four bowls connected together at various heights. Thanks to the Convic Crew for allowing us to work on it. We also joined in on a street course, and are now working on the pool that I believe will be up there with the best bowls in the world.

Meyer
Growing up in Hawaii, we designed and built several ramps and little parks. We actually did the design for the park they're building on the island right now. It's a Mickey Mouse bowl.

Mountain
I designed some of the first wood parks built. I've had a ramp since 1978. I built ramps so we would have something to skate. And at the time all the cement parks had gone out of business and no one was doing anything about it. I didn't like doing it. I just wanted to get the ball rolling with new ideas and designs. It was all new at that time — to build things out of wood. Get others to see the idea and go from there. It's been years. It hurts my back.

> You've got to battle the system straight out ... you have to fight for your right to skate.

Santarossa
Yes, I helped design the first Skate Street and the Santa Barbara Skatepark. I even drilled some screws at the old Skate Zone and at Skate Street.

How can riders get parks built where they live?

Alva
You've got to battle the system straight out. You have to go toe to toe with the government and the people that oppress you. You've

Skate on other people's property so much that the city has to do something about it.

got to go straight to the source, and if you want a free skateboard park in your community, you are going to have to go toe to toe with the city. It doesn't have to be a battle, maybe they'll cooperate with you, but I think in the long run you have to fight for your right to skate.

Badillo
Check out my chapter on building skateparks.

McDougall (Dorfus)
Approach your local council with a concept. Do background research on it, *i.e.*, location, design and budget, builders, talk about the success of other parks, anything you can think of to make it easier for them to say yes. If all else fails, build something yourself.

Meyer
Well, it's going to take some skaters getting in trouble first. Cops having a problem with kids skating here or there is usually the ticket for a park. But I think if a community really embraces skateboarding, they pop up for the good and right reasons. Take a look at Colorado or Canada. These communities love their skateparks and are very proud of them — and proud that they have the best. I think that's the great thing right there.

Mountain
Skate on other people's property so much that the city has to do something about it. Our cities build parks to hide a problem. That's why they are built the way they are. They

are the new judicial halls. Build it yourself or spend a lot of time trying to educate the city about something you love.

Santarossa
Bug your city council 'til their ears bleed.

Do anything to make them say yes.

influences

Name your influences.

Acuna

When I was growing up, all my friends were my biggest influences when it came to skateboarding. We all pushed each other to get better, but to also just have fun with it. So just skate for fun.

> Skate tough or go home.

Alva

Torger Johnson was probably the most influential skateboarder regarding my style, my direction and my approach to skateboarding. There were a few other guys like Danny Bearer and Davey Hilton. Some other guys I competed with like John Davison and Ross Powell. Some of the guys I skated against early were a heavy influence on me. Surfing had a lot of influence, too. Guys like Barry Kanaiaupuni and Reno Abellira. The surfers from Dogtown like Wayne Inouye, Jeff Ho, Bill Urbany, Jeff Sibley. A bunch of surfers had a lot of influence over the way I skated. Skate tough or go home.

Badillo

Tony Alva, Lance Mountain, John Cardiel, a lot of my friends like Dan Sabelis and others. But what inspires me is seeing skateboarding in kids. Watching the way kids embrace skateboarding.

Fletcher

Jason Jessee is probably one of the biggest influences in my skateboarding.

> What inspires me is seeing skateboarding in kids.

And Duane Peters. As a kid, I looked up to Duane because I was just super gnarly. I grew up with Jason so he was involved in that whole deal.

I'm influenced by attitudes ... not the way they skate.

McDougall (Dorfus)
When I was young I was influenced mostly by the people I skated with (still, to this day). I liked watching old Powell Peralta videos and then trying out all the tricks with my mates. Nowadays I am influenced by people's attitudes toward skating, not necessarily the way they skate. I am inspired by skating someone's back yard or something that a skater has built and knowing how proud he is of what he has accomplished. From the crappiest ramp to the gnarliest of bowls, the back yard is where I thrive.

Meyer
Mark Partain had more impact on my skateboarding and in and out of the water, than any other person I've met. He was a handful, and man, if you know him, well, he is your best friend. Partain can do anything on any terrain. The most comfortable, most consistent, most casual skater I've ever met.

Mountain
Tony Alva, Jay Adams, Stacy Peralta, most of the late '70s early '80s pros, Steve Cab, my team, Ray Barbee, Bob Burnquist, Rodrigo Tx. So many.

Mulder
Matt Hensley. He always sticks out in my memory as one of the best skaters. But there's too many — Mark Gonzales, Guy Mariano, Brian Lotti, Jovantae Turner, Wade Speyer ...

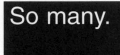**So many.**

Pastras
Tony Alva, Mark Gonzales, Geoff Rowley, Barker Barret, Mike Valley, Jason Lee, Roy Barbee and many, many more ...

Santarossa
Steve Caballero, Lance Mountain, Neil Blender, Brian Anderson, Donny Barley, Eric Koston, Mike Carrol, the list goes on ...

Ariel Shaw

Straight to the source

Since this book is for serious riders, we had to include one of the true originals. Tony Alva is widely considered to be among the most influential skaters in skateboarding history. His credentials are long and heavy (he invented this trick, the frontside air, in a Santa Monica pool nearly 30 years ago). But he in no way rests on his laurels. The fire yet burns and he skates and surfs hard each day. Lately he's been starring in theaters across the nation in the Stacy Peralta film *Dogtown and Z-Boys*. Together with Stacy, Tony has appeared on screen and in print bringing the skate message to America — *i.e.*, Skate tough or go home.

preflight

2 twenty-five tricks

The single purpose of the present moment is essential.

Clockwise from upper left: Mikey Pacheco, Todd Huber and Steve Chalme (with Steve Badillo). Mikey and Steve Chalme took the shots and Todd provided Skatelab. Thanks, guys!

airs

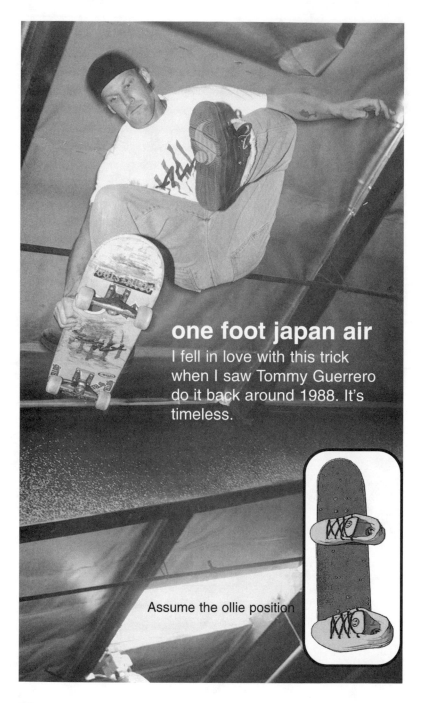

one foot japan air

I fell in love with this trick when I saw Tommy Guerrero do it back around 1988. It's timeless.

Assume the ollie position

Sequence by Mikey Pacheco

Approach the lip with great speed. Bend knees slightly and pop an ollie. As you start to fly, let your tail foot trail off the board and kick that foot out.

At the same time grab Japan with the lead (or mute) hand. Lay your front knee on the board in Japan position and hold.

Bring your tail foot back to the board while you are still skying.

Let go of the board as you land — leaning forward with feet spread. Now go play with your acoustic guitar.

backside 360 air

Assume the ollie position

Ride your wooden toy as fast as you can. Keep feet spread on top of your board. When you hit the lip, start to rotate your body backside 360 using head, shoulders and hips.

Grab the board behind you with the lead hand. Keep rotating all the way around. Look down and check out your landing area.

Just before you land, let go of the board. Flex knees and compress to absorb impact. Lean forward and ride it out.

frontside 360 air

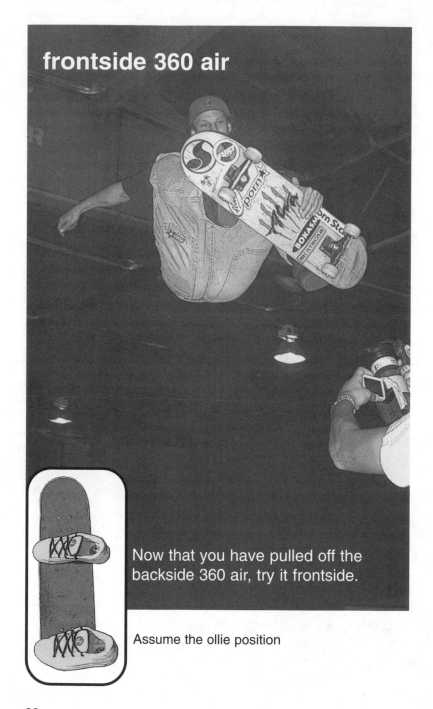

Now that you have pulled off the backside 360 air, try it frontside.

Assume the ollie position

Sequence by Mikey Pacheco

Once again ride up to the lip with as much speed as possible. Rotate your body frontside 360 using head, shoulders and hips.

Grab frontside with your rear (or indy) hand and rotate all the way around. Look down and make sure you have clear landing.

As you land, let go of the board and compress. Now try a 540!

sal flip

This trick was invented by Sal Barbier, hence the name.

Assume the ollie position

Sequence by Mikey Pacheco

Push the board as fast as it will go. Approach the lip bending your knees with your lead hand ready to grab the nose.

Grab the nose with your fingers on the grip tape side and your thumb on the bottom of the board. Start to flip the board into and underneath your body.

Keep knees up and over the board. Now rotate your body 180 as you rotate the finger flip 180. Spread feet over the bolts as you land.

You should be in the fakie position when you land. Lean in the direction your board is going. Remember to call up Sal and say thanks.

Behind the scene.

**pressure flip
mute grab**

Assume the kickflip position

Sequence by Steve Chalme

Ride as fast as you can. When you hit the lip, feet should be in pressure flip position. Your tail foot should be on the tip of the tail with toes along the outside edge. Your front foot should be in kickflip position but you are not going to kickflip the board. As you start to pressure flip, flip the board into your body.

Keep your front foot up and out of the way. Let the board rotate until you can grab it mute with your lead hand. Your feet should be spread as you grab mute.

Land it by putting your feet back on the board over the bolts. Let go and roll away. Now go tell your best friend that you skate better.

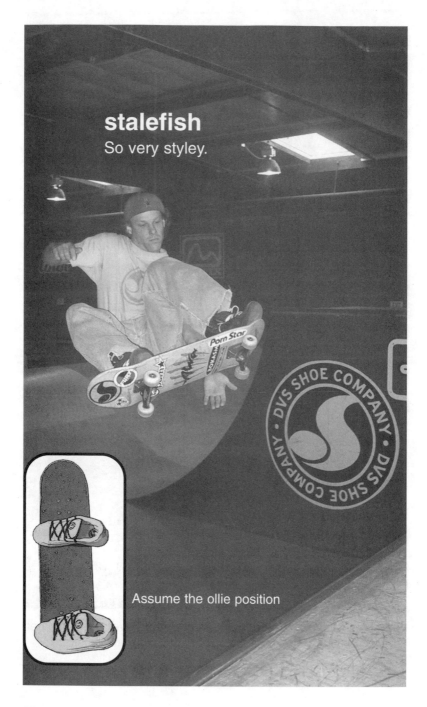

stalefish
So very styley.

Assume the ollie position

Sequence by Mikey Pacheco

Start by rolling up to the coping with lots of speed (the faster you go the higher the air). Bend knees and snap that ollie frontside.

Use your trailing hand to grab the board. Drop your hand behind and in between your legs to grab stalefish. When you grab, pull up and try to lay your knees down for style.

As you start to come back into the transition, extend your legs and let go of the board. Try to land just underneath the coping and lean forward. Ride it out and set up for your next trick.

frontside air

Tony Alva was the first
skater to do a frontside air.
This is for you T.A.

Assume the bolts position

Sequence by Mikey Pacheco

Skate up to the coping with plenty of speed. Bend your knees and keep your feet spread out on your board. Blast a frontside ollie and grab the board with your indy hand.

Float the air as long as you can. Turn the nose back into the transition as you let go of the board. Land with your knees compressing into the transition.

Stand up and say thanks T.A.

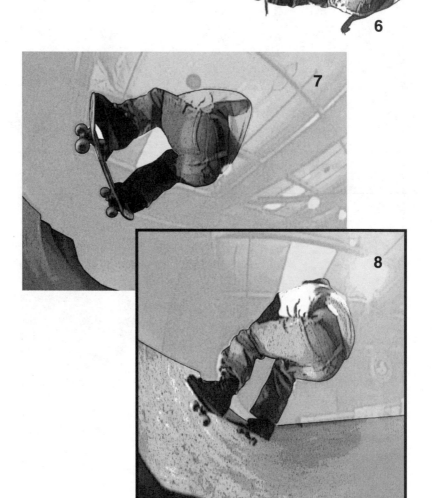

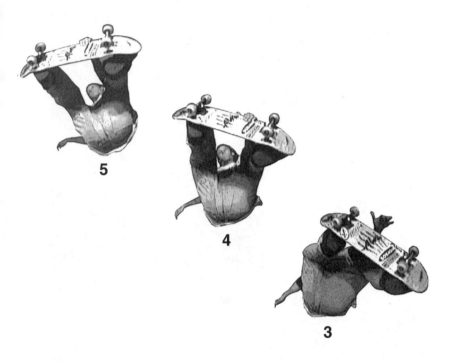

5

4

3

Lights, camera, action!

footwork

frontside flip

Assume the kickflip position

You can do this trick at almost any speed — even standing still. But the faster you go the higher and longer your frontside flip will be.

Sequence by Steve Chalme

Start with a speed comfortable for you. Bend knees and snap the frontside ollie. As you ollie, your front foot will go frontside as you kickflip.

Lift your knees up to allow the board to rotate underneath. At the same time rotate your body 180 in order to land fakie.

Place feet over the bolts and try to land on them. Straighten out and roll away fakie. Try it a thousand more times.

frontside halfcab kickflip

Assume the kickflip position

Sequence by Steve Chalme

Before you try this trick, you should be able to frontside halfcab ollie and kickflip. Start off riding fakie with feet in kickflip position. Rotate your body frontside as you snap a halfcab ollie.

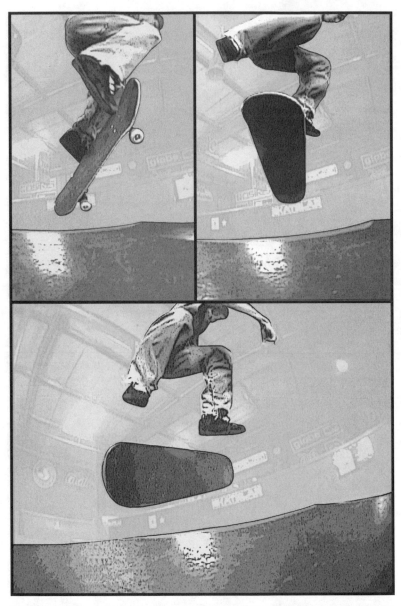

Kickflip the board keeping your knees high above the board so it can flip underneath. Keep rotating your body. Time your landing as the board finishes flipping around.

Try to land with feet spread over the bolts. When you land you should be facing forward with a smile on your face. Hip hip hooraayy!

ollie impossible

Assume the ollie impossible position

Mr. Rodney Mullen invented and perfected this trick. Try this trick on flat ground before trying it over a hip.

Ride up with moderate speed with your tail foot toes gripping the tail. The front foot should be near the nose and off to the side ready to come off the board. Snap an ollie and with your tail foot scoop the tail around your foot.

Tuck your knees up as the board flips beneath you. As the board comes around, try to land your front foot on top of the bolts. Ride away feeling like Rodney.

Impossible practice
Place the board on the ground. Put your tail foot on the tail with your toes gripping the tail. Put your front foot on the ground. Then scoop the board around 360 and try to land it one foot. Try this a few hundred times to understand the impossible part of the trick.

270 rewind grind

Assume the ollie position

This trick can go with liptricks or grinds 'n slides, but I wanted to show how to rotate your feet.

Sequence by Mikey Pacheco

Ride up to the lip with much needed speed. Hit the lip at a slight angle to carry the grind through. Pop your frontside ollie while rotating your tail foot 270 degrees.

Try to land your front truck on the coping first, then your back truck. You will be grinding switch 50/50. Ride out the switch 50/50 until you start to lose speed.

Now with your front foot (which is really your tail foot) push it into the transition and your tail foot will follow. Lean fakie and ride it out. Put your hands in the air like you don't care.

liptricks

frontside lipslide

A frontside lip-slide is a staple in the skater's bag of tricks.

Assume a wide stance

Approach the lip with as much speed as you can (the faster you go the longer you'll slide). Bend your knees as you ollie frontside.

Drift frontside facing the coping. Push the tail foot over the deck and keep centered over the board. Let it slide as far as it will go. When you start to come back into the transition, you need to bend your front knee and lean forward.

Push down on the nose with your lead foot so the back trucks can come in under the coping. Ride into the transition looking forward.

backside lipslide

Assume a wide stance

So styley and again should be one of your staples.

Sequence by Steve Chalme

Just like the frontside lipslide, approach the lip with as much speed as you can. Bend your knees as you ollie backside.

Drift backside to the coping. Swing your tail foot over the deck and keep yourself centered over the board. Twist your head around to see where you are going. Let it slide as far as it will go and remain centered over the board.

Look and lean back into the transition. Push down on the nose with your lead foot so your back trucks can come in under the coping. Ride into the transition looking straight ahead.

**backside
5-0 grind
to fakie**

Assume the bolts position

This trick can go with the grinds 'n slides section but to me it's always been more of a liptrick.

Sequence by Mikey Pacheco

Approach the coping with the need for speed. Lift your nose up by pushing down on the tail. At the same time, push your weight down on your back truck as you start to grind the coping.

Keep the nose up while staying centered over the back truck (this is the tricky part). Let it grind out, then turn the back truck into fakie position by pushing the truck into the transition.

Lean fakie, look forward and stand up. Roll away feeling good.

blunt pivot to fakie

Assume the bolts position

This is one of my favorite tricks. I first learned it as a grommet and landed it on a quarter bet.

Sequence by Steve Chalme

Ride straight up the transition with moderate speed. Keep your board vertical while going into the blunt (if you push the front of the board too much, you won't be able to ollie back into the transition).

Once you get the board into the blunt position, you need to ollie back into the transition like a blunt ollie. But as you ollie back in, smack your back truck to the pivot position. At the same time, crank the nose backside. Keep your body centered over the

back truck and start to lean back into the transition in the fakie position. As you start rolling down fakie, keep the nose up under the coping so you don't hang up. Turn your head and weight into the transition. You should be looking fakie.

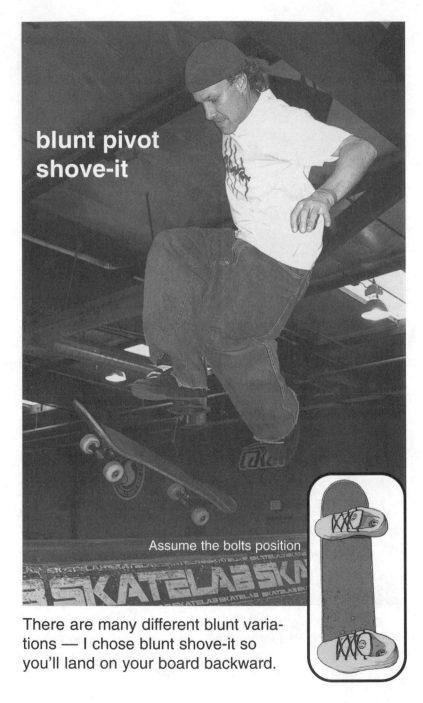

blunt pivot shove-it

Assume the bolts position

There are many different blunt variations — I chose blunt shove-it so you'll land on your board backward.

Ride straight up the transition with moderate speed. Keep your board vertical while going into the blunt (if you push the front of the board too much you won't be able to shove-it back into the transition).

Once you get the board into the blunt position, use your tail foot toes to grip around the tail. Now with both feet at the same time you are going to do a kind of airwalk move with your feet. That means you kick your front foot out toward the

coping and with your tail foot shove-it the board underneath you. Keep knees up and wait for the board to come around. Spread your feet as you land on the board. Land fakie, rock ...

... lean back into the transition, turn your head and look where you're going.

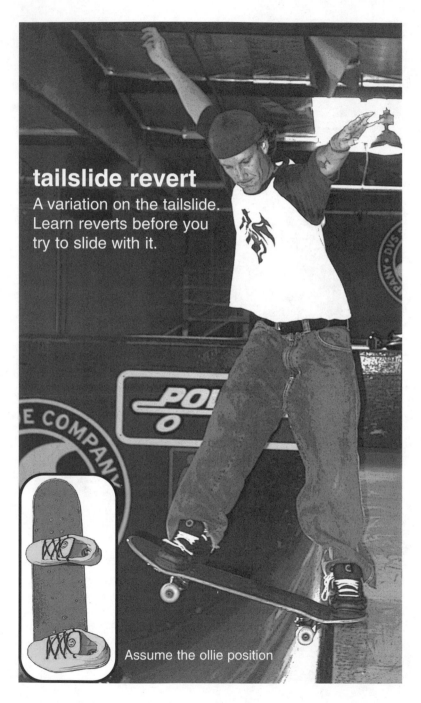

tailslide revert

A variation on the tailslide. Learn reverts before you try to slide with it.

Assume the ollie position

Sequence by Mikey Pacheco

Remember, the faster you approach the coping the farther you will tailslide. Ride or carve frontside up to the transition at an angle with lots of speed. Bend your knees, pop a small ollie and push your tail foot to the coping.

Once the tail is on the coping, stay centered over the board with most of your weight on the tail and let yourself slide as far as you can.

Swing shoulders and hips into the transition while pushing hard on the tail and letting your body come around 180 to fakie (revert position). Face forward and ride it through.

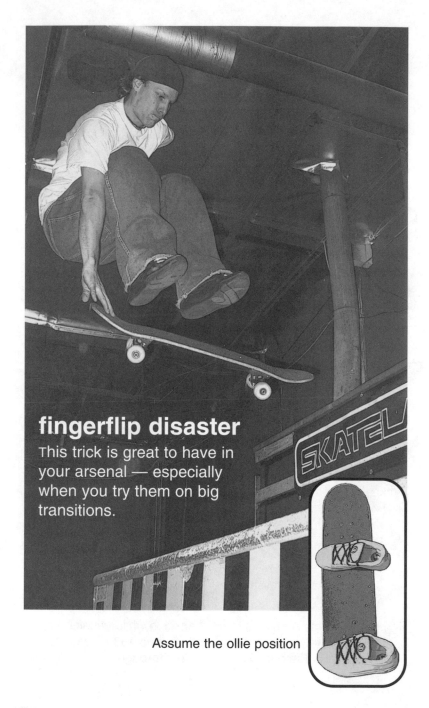

fingerflip disaster

This trick is great to have in your arsenal — especially when you try them on big transitions.

Assume the ollie position

Sequence by Steve Chalme

Approach the coping with moderate speed. Ride straight up the transition and pop off the coping. With your leading hand, grab the nose with fingers down and thumb up. Fingers should be on the grip tape and thumb underneath the nose.

As you ascend, start to flip the board into you. Bring knees up and around the board as it flips (keep your knees bent). As you come down, let go of the board, spread feet and land disaster on the bolts.

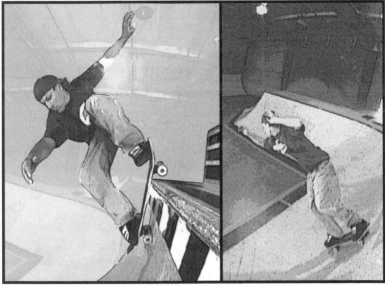

As you come back into the transition, press down on the nose so the back truck comes in under the coping. Keep your head forward and ride it out. Stoked.

Nosepick

Nosepick is old school and old school rocks.

Assume a wide stance

Sequence by Steve Chalme

Ride up the transition at a slight angle with moderate speed. Grab indy just below the coping. Pull up on the nose and at the same time pull up with your indy hand.

Now smack down your front truck on the coping. Now you are going to indy air back into the transition.

Let go of the board, stand up and ride it out. Face forward.

grinds 'n slides

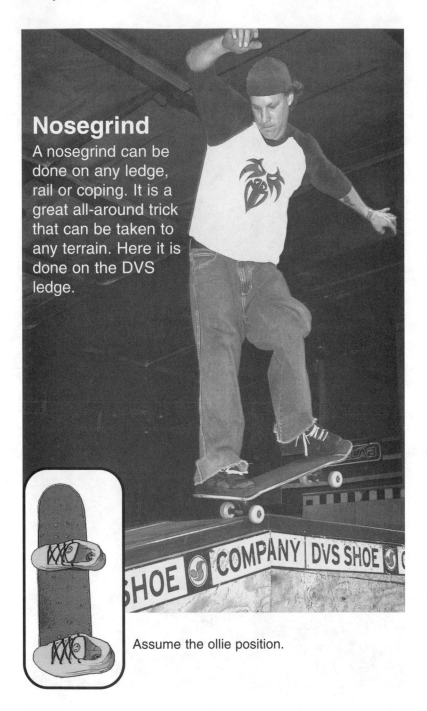

Nosegrind

A nosegrind can be done on any ledge, rail or coping. It is a great all-around trick that can be taken to any terrain. Here it is done on the DVS ledge.

Assume the ollie position.

146

Sequence by Steve Chalme

Approach the ledge with moderate speed in the ollie position with front foot just below the bolts. Bend your knees and snap an ollie pulling your front foot up toward the nose. Push the nose down to the ledge in the nosegrind position keeping your back foot on the tail.

Balance the nosegrind on the ledge by keeping your arms out and head up.

As you approach the end, lean forward clearing your back truck from the ledge. Land it with feet spread and head held high. Nice.

feeble grind 180 out

Assume the ollie position.

Sequence by Mikey Pacheco

You should be able to do feeble grinds before you try to 180 out. Skate up to the rail at a slight angle with plenty of speed. Bend your knees and pop an ollie. Ollie high enough to land on top of the rail.

With your tail foot, grind the rail in feeble position. At the same time, point your front foot into smith position laying down the edge of the board on the rail. Stay centered over the board and let it grind out.

When you get to the end of the rail, swing your shoulders and hips frontside 180. Your feet will follow your hips and shoulders. Land it with your feet spread and roll away.

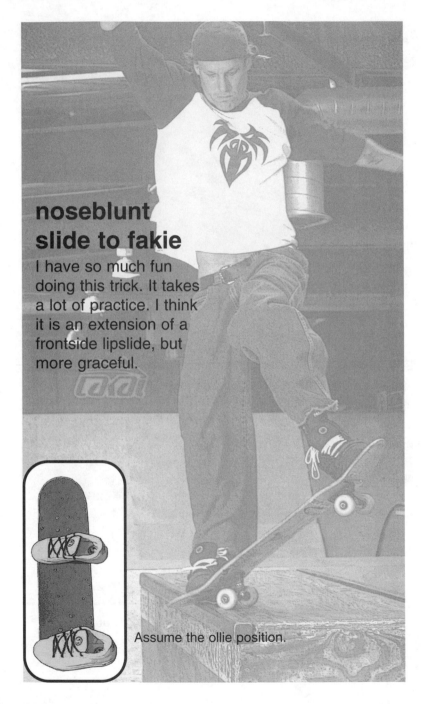

noseblunt slide to fakie

I have so much fun doing this trick. It takes a lot of practice. I think it is an extension of a frontside lipslide, but more graceful.

Assume the ollie position.

154

Sequence by Steve Chalme

Skate up to the ledge at high speed. Bend your knees and ollie big enough to sky over the ledge. With your front foot, pull the nose around to the ledge in the blunt position.

Keep your weight on the front nose. Let it slide along the ledge.

As you start to get to the end, swing your tail foot around to the fakie position. Land on your bolts going fakie. Stand up and be happy.

halfcab
noseslide

This trick can go with
liptricks or grinds 'n
slides, but I wanted
to show how to rotate
your feet.

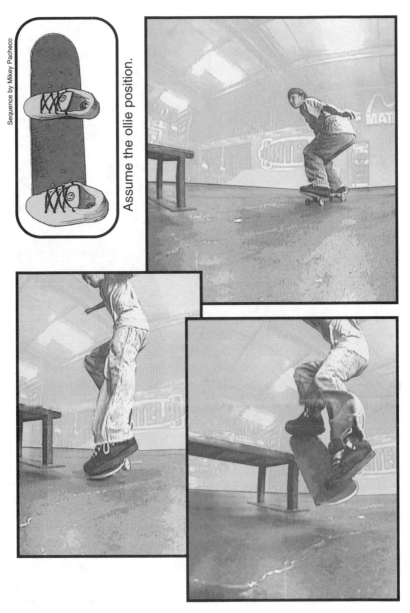

Sequence by Mikey Pacheco

Assume the ollie position.

To begin this trick you need to be riding fakie. Bend your knees as you start to ollie halfcab. Snap the tail and pull the nose around to the ledge. Land on top of your noseslide with most of your weight on the nose.

Stay centered over the nose and let it slide out.

When you get to the end of the ledge, start to push your front foot forward and your tail foot behind you. You should land it coming off normal, leaning forward and feeling great.

**180
nosegrind
180 out**

Assume the ollie position

This trick takes lots of practice. Ride up to the ledge going fast and ready to commit all the way. Pull a big frontside 180 ollie. Land your front truck on top of the ledge.

You should be in switch 5-0 position as you grind down the ledge. Most of your weight should be on the nosegrind until you get to the end of the ledge.

At that point, start to swing your tail foot around 180 as you push your front foot forward to land 180. Lean forward as you ride away and shout *Yeah! I pulled it!*

**switch
noseslide
270
shove-it
out**

Assume the ollie position

Sequence by Mikey Pacheco

You must be able to ride and ollie switch. Approach the ledge with plenty of speed. Bend your knees and switch ollie keeping your front foot (which is really your tail foot) on the nose. Land on the ledge switch noseslide.

Stay centered over your board with most of your weight on the nose. Let it slide as far as you can go. As you start to reach the end of the ledge, curl your front foot toes around the nose to shove-it out.

Start by pushing the nose around and at the same time lifting your feet up while the board spins 270. As the board is spinning, switch your body position back to normal.

You should land back on your board riding away in the normal foot that you are. For me (if you can't tell by now) it's goofy.

Build a park in your town / Steve Badillo

Skaters have been building ramps, cement bowls and obstacles for nearly a half century, but today's rate of skatepark creation is unparalled. International Association of Skateboard Companies (IASC) predicts that more that 1,000 parks will be up and running by summer of 2002. Now is the time to get the park you want in your city.

In general, skateparks are built either privately or publically. Sometimes people use their own money to purchase the materials and labor needed to create private parks. Other times cities build public parks with taxpayer money. I'll briefly outline these two ways parks get built and managed.

It's vital to note that skaters can endure tough measures and long waits to get their parks built. It takes persistence and the will to succeed to see your dreams come true. Try to create your park with the services of an established professional skatepark building crew. Most of these builders are skaters themselves and know how to satisfy skater needs. The good ones are more than builders. They are artists.

**at a glance:
action points
for private parks**
1. Location
2. Buy or lease?
3. Check with city for
   codes
4. Insurance
5. Professional skatepark
   building crew
6. Wood or concrete?
7. Customize your park
8. Staff of workers

**Privately owned
skateparks**
First, find a good place to build. Location is important because skateparks are very noisy and crowded with skaters. An ideal place would be some type of warehouse away from residential neighborhoods. You can either buy the warehouse or lease it. If you lease, make sure it's a long lease and it's a long lease and that you have the option to renew. You have to check with the city to see if the warehouse is up to code for the project. This means a fire marshal must check it out. Next, you need insurance. Insurance is relatively easy to get but takes a lot of money.

Once you have location, an OK from the city and insurance, it's time to build. Make sure you hire a professional skatepark building crew. There are many crews out there and a list of some of the best is in the resources section. Decide if you wish to build a wood or concrete park. I personally like both types. A wood park will need more maintenance than a concrete park, but a wood park can keep changing with new ideas over the years. A concrete park is permanent.

After the park has been built, you can enhance your investment a number of ways. Consider putting in a

Wood underneath a roof. Skatelab. Simi Valley, California.

pro shop that sells gear, repair services and appropriate
retail items. You may want to round out the environ-
ment by adding a skater's lounge, vending machines,
video games and a stage for bands or other events.
You'll have to hire a staff to work the front desk and
pro shop and to maintain the ramps. Don't forget to
find a local pro skater to teach beginners. When everything's in place, run the park like a regular business
and charge kids to skate. One more suggestion: the
bigger the park the better! Invite me to the Grand
Opening. Good luck!

at a glance:
action points
for public parks
1. Select a leader
2. Petition signatures
3. Location
4. City council meetings
5. Wood or concrete?
6. Funding
7. Professional skatepark building crew
8. Grand opening

Public skateparks

Building a public skatepark is totally different. First and foremost, you will need someone or a group of people to stay with this project as long as it lasts — it may take a few years to get the city to approve and build it. The key person or people selected will then need to petition the city. This means they must pass around a petition and collect signatures from skateboarders, parents, teachers and local citizens to pressure and convince the city to build a public skatepark. The more signatures the better.

Next, it's up to you and your group to find possible locations for the park. You need to present multiple sites so the city has options to consider.

With signatures and locations in hand, it's time to attend council meetings. Most cities have council meetings once a month which you need to attend each time. Show up with everyone that wants to be involved — skaters, parents, local homeowners, teachers and business owners. At the council meeting stand tall and explain your ideas, present signatures and introduce the backers you brought with you.

Tell the council that if they build a skatepark they'll

Concrete outside. Robb Field. San Diego, California.

provide a safe place for kids to go that will keep them off the streets. A skatepark will also keep kids from skating public places such as banks, malls, downtown streets and shopping areas. Give the city the option for a wood park or a concrete park. Most cities build concrete parks because they are cheaper and require less maintenance than wood parks.

Remember that the leaders in charge of this project must go to every city council meeting to keep the pressure on. Once the council has approved the project, they'll decide where to build the park and most importantly, how to build the park. The city needs to find funding to support the park — often money budgeted through the Parks and Recreation Department.

Again, strongly advise the council to hire a professional skatepark building crew. Also suggest that the skatepark be free and open to the public. Remember city councils are slow to take action. It's important to be patient!

Wood parks can be altered to incorporate new ideas.

Concrete, on the other hand, is permanent yet easier and less expensive to maintain.

like a clubhouse

Going out on a limb
with Todd Huber
of Skatelab Skatepark
Simi Valley, California

**Tell me about
creating Skatelab.**
The way that this park
came to be was, first we
approached the city, but
there was no interest. Then
we tried the YMCA, and
there was no interest.
Finally, it was a matter of a
bunch of friends who
pooled their resources.
There were just the right combination of people and
resources, and that's what made it happen. I think that
you probably have to mess around with the mix a little
bit, depending on who you are and where you are and
the group of people that you're doing it with to make
it happen.

We kind of just threw it all in the pot and we were
lucky that it came out good. There were a lot of factors
that could have gone either way. We had just a few
more that went for us instead of against us. I think
that's why we were able to pull it off. The factors that
went against us were ones that we were able to get
past. Like neighbors that were concerned about what

We thought that we were going to be able to just call up the guy who was renting the building and give him our rent and start building our ramps. But it wasn't like that at all.

was going to go on here. That was really the main thing. We just had some good luck on top of it all.

What are the specific problems you have creating a private park?
I think finding the right spot.

You mentioned that neighbors were a problem?
They weren't a problem. They just wanted to know what was going to happen. They wanted to make sure that it wasn't going to be a problem. One couple's been there their whole life, for 30 years, and they wanted to keep it quiet in the neighborhood and so do we. We close at 10 o'clock so it's no big deal. They just had questions, you know.

Did you have to go in front of a council?
Oh, yeah. We had to go in front of a lot of councils.

Really? Even though it's a private park?
Yeah. No matter what you're doing you have to get a special use permit. Just like a bowling alley, you have to get a special use permit. At least in this town. I don't know about any other towns.

You had to get approval from the city to build a skatepark?
Yeah, and we did. There was no reason not to approve it. What was the difference between a skatepark or a roller rink or whatever? What does it matter? That's the approach we took. What's the difference? You should be able to do whatever you want.

How long did the whole process take?
Over a year.

Did it surprise you that it took so long?
I think we were naive because we thought that we were going to be able to just call up the guy who was renting the building and give him our rent and start building our ramps. But it wasn't like that at all.

So the big obstacle was getting permission and going through all the red tape with the city?
Yeah. You know, there were obstacles, but none of them were too hard to overcome, like the neighbors, for example.

If you did it over again, how would you organize yourself better? How would you approach the whole thing? Or does it just take year? Is it like giving birth ... it takes almost a year? (laughter)
I've gotta say that every city is probably different. I think it depends on the need in the town and the council people. Like we had a council lady that was ... I mean, we were having trouble getting things signed off. You had to get things signed off by every agency in town — the police, the fire marshal, public works, building and safety — all have to come and inspect the

> There's isn't a little pamphlet that says *Okay, first you find a building and then you make sure the building is zoned ...* You just don't know. It was all trial and error ... and it still is.

project and sign you off before you can open. We were having trouble getting a lot of them, and this one council lady picked me up, took me to City Hall and walked me through all departments. I got like about five out of six in one day. I had been struggling. It's a hard thing if you've never done it before.

I think usually ... like say if you're going to open a Jack in the Box— I think they usually hire a firm that specializes in that sort of thing — to deal with the city. They know what to do, know the permits that are needed, know the questions that are going to be asked. But if you've never done it before it's very difficult.

You didn't know where to begin ...
There isn't a little pamphlet that says *Okay, first you find a building and then you make sure the building is zoned ...* You just don't know. It was all trial and error and it still is.

Actually, I don't want to give away too many of my secrets. I think that the info I learned is sort of valuable now, because I can help other people and I just don't want to like give all my secrets away ...

Not that I'm too worried about it ... I'm just saying that
I get so many people who ask me about building parks.
It's really a time issue. If you have 10 people a week
who say *I'm thinking about opening this park* ... I just
can't help them all. What do you do?

Well, there's a lot of information online.
That's true. But I guess what I'm saying is that my time
... I just barely have enough time to deal with the kids
who come in. You know what I mean? We're really a
small-time thing. We only have 8 or 10 employees. It's
like a clubhouse. I mean, that's our approach. So it's
hard for me to give too much of ... I mean, like I sort of
want to forget about all that ... you know? Like we're
talking about it now and it's bringing up bad memories
(laughter). It was a hard time. Like I said, we thought it
was going to be really easy. Just pay the rent, open the
door, no big deal. Now that I'm done with it, I just
don't want to have anything to do with that process
again.

I wish somebody would come up and say *Hey, we're
serious. I started Game Works and I want to start one
of these Skatelabs. I like your concept and I want to
do one of these in every major city.* I think that would
be great. I would be into that. But I don't want to be
the guy to hustle it. Do this thing like the Johnny
Appleseed of skateparks. You know, go around and
spread all the knowledge. I'm not that guy. You have to
go on the internet for that — skatepark.org is a good
one. They have lots of things.

People are going to get into it for the wrong reasons. Like ESPN. Who knows how interested they really are in skate parks. I think of ESPN like with baseball games. It just doesn't seem right.

Are there skatepark franchises out there?
Yeah. Vans has like about 11 skateparks. ESPN is opening skateparks. It's almost a joke in a way. I mean, when we were kids there were skateparks everywhere and they all died because there were too many of them, in my opinion. Everyone says it's the liability or the design, but there were just too many skateparks. If you have a skatepark in every town and they get better and better and better, they're not all going to survive. That's sort of my take on it. People always say *Oh, no! You can never have enough skateparks ... there's enough skaters out there!* That's baloney. It's going to go up and down, and up and down ...

I think the more skateparks there are, the worse it's going to get. I think there should be a few great parks and there should be a few public parks. If there gets to be too many, I don't think we're all going to survive. I don't think anyone is going to survive. If there are ten more parks like this within two hours from here, like there used to be, and they are all killer ... there aren't enough people to support them. That's what happened

back when things were a lot cheaper and stuff. That's
my theory about skateparks. I think ... oh, man, I don't
know what the word is ... it's just that history is going
to repeat itself.

So you think there might be a slowdown?
I don't know. I'm going out on a limb by saying that
because some other people have told me that I'm dead
wrong. But I think that's wishful thinking. I'm just
trying to be honest with myself. I'm the most opti-
mistic guy there is. I don't want ... I can't imagine
doing anything else. But I'm just being real. I think
people are going to get into it for the wrong reasons.
Like ESPN. Who knows how interested they really are
in skateparks. I think of ESPN like with baseball games.
It just doesn't seem right to me ... I don't know...

Well, they're big corporations ...
Yeah, I don't know. It doesn't seem like the same thing.
That's an example of what I think is going to happen
with those kind of places all around. It's just going to
suck eventually. It might be six to eight years before it
happens. I could be wrong. Like we've been here for
four years and no one has challenged us. But I think
they're gonna. I don't know. But I'm ready for it.

what you can do

Help build a strong, united skatepark-creation committee with influential members of your community.

Help find several location possibilities with good substructure, near public transportation and major population centers.

Help create a vision of your skatepark and share it with the decision makers and everyone else.

Insist that a budget be allocated that truly fulfills your vision. Research skatepark projects of other cities and supply your decision makers with facts and figures.

Insist that decision makers hire a designer who skates. Help the city find one.

Insist that skaters be involved with the process from start to finish. Skaters should study and approve the designs and review stages of the construction. Skaters, as a unified front, should study the plans and make themselves available and useful to decision makers.

Insist that decision makers hire a contractor based on experience, reputation and level of service. Help the city find skatepark builders.

Show up at all the meetings and be ready to work. Be patient and courteous and persistent with decision makers. Create a strong, positive bond with each of them. Help the decision makers by supplying them with plenty of information about skating and skateparks.

Best parks / Steve Badillo

Here's a guide to some of the best skateparks in Colorado and Oregon — actually the whole USA. Many people in these states have helped me on various road-trips and this is my way of saying thanks to those who have stoked me when I skated through their town.

colorado

If you and your buddies are thinking of going on a skate trip, I would suggest the great state of Colorado. It has some of the biggest and best skateparks in America — rivaled only by Oregon. There are many more skateparks in Colorado than the ones I mention, but these are the ones I frequently visit. For much of the year snow is everywhere including inside the bowls, so travel from May–September for best conditions. Gather your sleeping bag, warm clothes, gas money, beef jerky and pads. Let's go to our first stop.

Grand Junction

When driving into Colorado from the west you will be on Interstate 70 to the outskirts of Grand Junction. It's a small town, but the kids are some of the coolest in Colorado. All the skaters (from as far away as Chino) like to check out the latest demo crew that comes through. Grand Junction is a cement outdoor skatepark and has a keyhole bowl that's at least 10 feet deep. It also has a square bowl spine that leads into an L-shape halfpipe. There's a street section that is less than good with only a fly box and a quarter pipe. Pads are not required and skating is free. A market is located nearby for food and drinks. The locals make this a stop worth going to and hanging

Montrose. Wrex. Frontside air.

out. Grand Junction is located on Orchard Avenue. *Next stop Montrose.*

Montrose
This is one of my favorite stops. It's an outdoor cement park, free to skate and you don't have to wear pads. Montrose is a very small town but they have a big skatepark. It's got a donut-shape volcano and a round bowl with an open end that leads to a big bank. A tear-shaped island leads the way to a million different lines. This is a must-visit skatepark. It's located a bit away from the town, so bring water.
Next stop Crested Butte.

Crested Butte

This park is located in the snowboard town of Crested Butte. It's an outdoor cement skatepark that's free to skate, but helmets are required. Cops do come around looking to give out tickets if you don't wear your helmet. This park has a huge open-end square bowl

with rounded corners. Its open end leads to a spine halfpipe that has round corner ends. This park also has round hips on both sides to blast airs. There's a street course with two banks, a fly box with a rail and a small ledge. This

Crested Butte. Wrex. Invert.

beautiful town is surrounded by huge mountains and downtown offers plenty of pizza and cold drinks. Crested Butte skatepark is located at 126 Elk Street. *Next stop Salida.*

Salida

If you are in the mood to skate a clover type bowl, this is the place. Salida is an outdoor cement skatepark. It's free to skate but you have to wear pads. It features a clover bowl but one end is square with round corners. Another end is round and the last end is a halfpipe. It's a great place to get your bowl session in. There's a river nearby where you can swim after skating. Salida also features a great contest every summer. The park is

located at 200 West First Street.
Next stop Breckenridge.

Breckenridge

Another snowboard town with rippers in the skatepark
and on the mountains. This is an outdoor cement

Steve Badillo

skatepark that's
free to skate but
you have to wear
a helmet. It has a
square bowl with
an open end that
leads into a kind
of snake run half-
pipe. There's a
tear-shaped island
spine that's great
for transfers.
There's also a
street course

Breckenridge. Dorfus. Tailtap transfer.

that's a little bit better than some of the other street
courses we've reviewed. It has a fun box, banks,
quarter pipe, a rail and an L-shaped quarterpipe wall.
Next stop Silverthorne.

Silverthorne

This place is only about 20 minutes from Breckenridge
so if you visit Breckenridge, stop by Silverthorne, too.
Silverthorne has a great street course with pyramid,
half-bowl launcher, long ledge, tranny walls with pool
coping, escalating coping and big hips. This skatepark is
an outdoor cement park and is free to skate. You must
wear at least a helmet — I know because I was almost
ticketed by the local police. Silverthorne also has a

square bowl spine that leads into the street course — a good place to blast big air transfers. This park is located in a public park next to a library. *Next stop Denver.*

Denver

There are a few skateparks in Denver, but I'm talking about the Vans park. Vans is an indoor cement and wood skatepark. You have to pay and pads are required. They have a cement bowl and a really good wood street course. This park is like other Vans parks, complete with a pro shop, food and drinks. *Next stop Boulder.*

Silverthorne. Wrex. Just cruising.

Boulder

This is another city that has a couple of skateparks, but this is the main public park. It's free to skate this outdoor cement skatepark, but you have to wear pads. This park has it all — a huge round bowl that leads into a square bowl that leads into a square bowl spine into another square bowl. The street course is big with a pyramid and rail. It also has big walls that spit you out all over this place. You can transfer into and out of the bowls and street course. This is definitely a must on your journey through Colorado.
Next stop Aspen.

Aspen

Tim Payne built this park and anything Tim builds is a favorite of mine. This skatepark is an outdoor cement park and free to skate, but you must wear your helmet if you don't want to get hassled. This park is smooth with a nice reddish-brown cement finish. It has a sweet clover bowl that's square in the deep end and round in the two other bowls. The street course has inter-connecting spine capsules with a big 9-foot wall with pool coping that spits you out to a bank. Do yourself a favor and skate Aspen Skatepark.

Steve Badillo

Boulder. Yancy Meyer.
Frontside kickflip indy grab.

This is the last stop on my tour guide of Colorado. So get your friends together, pack up the car and get ready for a gnarly skate trip in the Rockies.

oregon

I've toured Oregon many times and new skateparks are popping up like mushrooms on your front lawn. There are many parks in this state, but I'm going to review only those I like to skate. In Oregon it rains much of the year so you should visit from May–September for best conditions. Gas up, put on your favorite shades, get some sunflower seeds and get ready for a West Coast trip Oregon-style. This is the land of giant skateparks, so bring your pads. Let's go to our first stop.

Ashland
When driving to Oregon from California you will be on Interstate 5. The first stop is Ashland just over the state line. This park is an outdoor cement skatepark and free to skate, but you must wear your pads. There's a cement round bowl that leads into another capsule bowl that leads into a snake run. That snake run leads into the street course. At the other end of the street course there is another small bowl. The street course has a pyramid, a ledge and a tombstone. If you blast out of the big bowl you can try to ride the tombstone wall. There are a couple of fun transfers here, especially from bowl to bowl. This is a perfect place to start your road trip. Ashland Skatepark is located at the corner of Hershey and Water streets. *Next stop Talent.*

Talent
This skatepark is not far from Ashland and halfway to Medford. Talent is an outdoor cement skatepark and you have to wear your pads. Cops are always hanging around watching for the unsuspecting skateboarder

with no helmet. This place has a square bowl with round corners right next to a round bowl that spines into the street course. The street course has a big bank wall where you can blast from the square bowl and a pyramid, too. One corner of the park is very unique — it has a quarterpipe that launches you up to the next level of transitions. There are many, many different lines in this part of the park. Talent Skatepark is located at East Main and Front streets. Check it out. *Next stop Medford.*

Medford

Our last stop in southern Oregon is Medford. There are a couple of skateparks in this town, but we want to go to Bear Creek Park. This is an outdoor cement park and you don't have to wear your pads. I skated this place right after it was built and had a memorable session. It has a cement bowl, a snake run with a tombstone and a street course with big banks and a big pyramid. Good flowing lines can be drawn here. *Next stop Burnside.*

Burnside Projects

This is the gnarliest skatepark in Oregon, not so much for the park itself, but because of the skaters who rule it. Be ready to throw down your best moves at Burnside. It's an outdoor cement skatepark and no gear is required. The best skaters in Oregon skate here and they maintain it. It was built by Red and his crew. Red has built many skateparks in Oregon, three of which are on my list. It has a big round cement bowl, a square bowl, huge hips, a killer vert wall, skateable vert corners, a street course and more. Burnside is featured in Tony Hawk's Pro Skater 1 and it comes pretty close to the real deal. This park is a must-skate place when vis-

Steve Badillo

Burnside. Dorfus.
Backside alley-oop ollie.

Jason Badillo

Newberg.

iting Oregon. Long live Burnside and the skaters who live there. Burnside is located under the Burnside Bridge. *Next stop Newberg.*

Newberg

This has to be one of the best skateparks in Oregon and another built by Red and his crew. It's an outdoor cement park and you don't have to wear pads, but I would advise that you do. There are so many transfers and hips it blows your mind. You will never run out of lines here — every time you skate you will find a new one to draw. It has to be one of the biggest parks — 28,000 square feet to be exact. There's a cement vert ramp that leads to corners and hips, a dragon rail with humps and a round volcano —all very cool. You

Two views of Lincoln City.

should stay a couple of days to get the most out of this park. Newberg is located at 1201 Blaine Street. *Next stop Lincoln City.*

Lincoln City
Lincoln City is yet another creation from Red and his crew. It's an outdoor cement skatepark and no pads are required. Did I mention it's also free to skate? There's a deep square bowl with a 5-foot tombstone that I saw Dorfus backside disaster. A snake run leads to the lower half of the park. There are several different transfers and hips to be conquered. When you're done skating, there's a casino nearby if you're feeling lucky. Lincoln City is located on the coast of Oregon and is the last stop on my tour of Oregon.

That's it. Get your crew together for the concrete and beauty that Oregon has to offer. I hope to see you when I'm traveling through Oregon and Colorado.

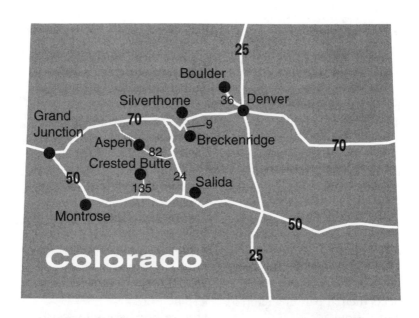

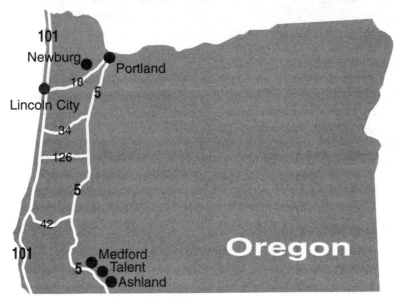

Colorado and Oregon tours.
Numbers represent highways. Maps show general location
information and are not to scale. You will need a road map.

Terms for terrain

Capsule bowl: A bowl in the shape of a capsule or pill.
Clover bowl: Three round bowls connected by the shallow end of a bowl.

Donut-shaped volcano: A donut-shaped cement ramp on top of a volcano-shaped cement pillar.

Escalating Coping: Where the coping follows a 45-degree angle along the top of a ramp. Escalating coping usually connects the flat part of a ramp to a tombstone.

Fly box: Where a launch ramp or bank ramp is connected to a box with a flat bank to land on.

Halfpipe: Two quarterpipes joined together with a flat bottom.
Hip: Where two perpendicular transitions or banks meet.

Keyhole: A type of bowl that looks like a round bowl with a roll-in channel.

L-shaped halfpipe: A halfpipe in the shape of an L with a hip and a corner.

Pyramid: Three or four bank ramps coming together to form a pyramid.

Quarterpipe: One transition ramp with coping.

Snake run: A winding cement path that usually ends in a bowl.
Spine capsules: Two capsule bowls joined in the middle with a spine.
Square bowl spine: A square bowl with a spine connected to it.

Tombstone: A large vertical extension from the halfpipe.
Transfer: When you air out of one ramp or bowl into another.

Vert Corners: The corners of square bowls with vertical walls.

Glossary

Backside: Riding a ramp, lip or ledge with your back facing the coping as you skate forward.

Blunt position: When your wheels are on top of the coping with the board in a vertical position and the tail flat on the transition.

Bolts: The hardware that keep your trucks on the skateboard.

Coping: The metal pipe that you grind located on top of the ramp.

Deck: Either the wooden platform of your skateboard or the horizontal platform at the top of a ramp.

Feeble position: Going backside with your back truck locked up on the coping with the nose pointing above the coping and your front leg straightened.

50/50 grind: Riding or grinding both trucks along a coping.

Frontside: Riding a ramp, lip or ledge with your chest facing the coping as you skate forward.

Indy hand: Back or tail hand that you grab the skateboard with.

Goofy foot: Stance where right foot is placed near the nose and left foot on the tail.

Grab: When you grab your board with any hand.

Grind: To ride your trucks along the coping.

Lip: Where the coping lays on the ramp. The lip of the ramp is where the coping is.

Mute hand: Lead or front hand that you grab the skateboard with.

Old School: A style of skating done before you were born.

Regular foot: Stance where left foot is placed near the nose and right foot on the tail.

Revert: To rotate your skateboard and body 180 degrees on transitions.

Smith position: Going frontside with your back truck locked up on the coping with the nose pointing below the coping and your front leg straightened.

Switch: Riding your skateboard backward.

Trucks: The hanger that holds your wheels.

Transition: The curved part of a ramp stretching from the flat bottom to the coping.

Bibliography

Baccigaluppi, John. *Declaration of Independents*. San Francisco, California: Chronicle Books, 2001.

Baum, Kenneth. *The Mental Edge*. New York, New York: Perigee Books, 1999.

Bermudez, Ben. *Skate! The Mongo's Guide to Skateboarding*. New York, New York: Cheapskate Press, 2001.

Borden, Ian. *Skateboarding, Space and the City.* New York, New York: Berg, 2001.

Brooke, Michael. *The Concrete Wave: The History of Skateboarding.* Toronto, Ontario: Warwick Publishing, 1999.

Davis, James. *Skateboard Roadmap*. England: Carlton Books Limited, 1999.

Hawk, Tony. *Hawk*. New York, New York: Regan Books, 2001.

Skateboarding Business. Oceanside, California: Transworld Media.

The New Yorker. New York, New York: The Conde Nast Publications, 7-1999.

Thrasher. *Insane Terrain*. New York, New York: Universe Publishing, 2001. Transworld Skateboarding. Oceanside, California: Transworld Magazine Corporation, 1-2000.

Resources

In alphabetical order we have a healthy dose of info about skateboarding as it relates to:

Books
Camps
Magazines
Museums
Organizations
Public skateparks (building of)
Shops
Skateparks (finding one)
Television
Web sites
Videos

For a quick fix go to **www.skateboarding.com** — this is an informative (but not the only) portal into the skateboarding galaxy. For face-to-face find a real skateboard shop and talk to real skaters.

Books
Books discovered on **amazon.com** and **barnesandnoble.com**.

Baccigaluppi, John. *Declaration of Independents*. San Francisco, California: Chronicle Books, 2001.

Bermudez, Ben. *Skate! The Mongo's Guide to Skateboarding*. New York, New York: Cheapskate Press, 2001.

Borden, Ian. *Skateboarding, Space and the City*. New York, New York: Berg, 2001.

Brooke, Michael. *The Concrete Wave: The History of Skateboarding*. Toronto, Ontario: Warwick Publishing, 1999.

Burke, L.M. *Skateboarding! Surf the Pavement*. New York, New York: Rosen Publishing Group, Inc., 1999.

Davis, James. *Skateboard Roadmap*. England: Carlton Books Limited, 1999.

Gould, Marilyn. *Skateboarding*. Mankato, Minnesota: Capstone Press, 1991.

Gutman, Bill. *Skateboarding: To the Extreme*. New York, New York: Tom Doherty Associates, Inc., 1997.

Hawk, Tony. *Hawk*. New York, New York: Regan Books, 2001.

Powell, Ben. *Extreme Sports: Skateboarding*. Hauppauge, New York: Barron's Educational Series, Inc. 1999.

Riggins, Edward. *Ramp Plans*. San Francisco, California: High Speed Productions, 2000.

Ryan, Pat. *Extreme Skateboarding*. Mankato, Minnesota: Capstone Press, 1998.

Shoemaker, Joel. *Skateboarding Streetstyle*. Mankato, Minnesota: Capstone Press, 1995.

Thrasher. *Insane Terrain*. New York, New York: Universe Publishing, 2001.

Camps
Donny Barley Skate Camp
1747 West Main Road
Middletown, Rhode Island
02842
401-848-8078

Lake Owen
HC 60 Box 60
Cable, Wisconsin 54821
715-798-3785

Magdalena Ecke Family YMCA
200 Saxony Road
Encinitas, California 92023-0907
760-942-9622

Mission Valley YMCA
5505 Friars Road
San Diego, California 92110
619-298-3576

Skatelab
Steve Badillo Skate Camp
4226 Valley Fair Street
Simi Valley, California 93063
805-578-0040
vtaskate@aol.com

Snow Valley
PO Box 2337
Running Springs, California
92382
909-867-2751

Visalia YMCA
Sequoia Lake, California
211 West Tulare Avenue
Visalia, California 93277
559-627-0700

Woodward Camp
Box 93
Route 45
Woodward, Pennsylvania 16882
814-349-5633

Young Life Skate Camp
Hope, British Columbia, Canada
604-807-3718

Magazines
Big Brother
www.bigbrothermagazine.com

Skateboarder
Surfer Publications
PO Box 1028
Dana Point, California 92629

Thrasher
High Speed Productions
1303 Underwood Avenue
San Francisco, California 94124
415-822-3083
www.thrashermagazine.com

Transworld Skateboarding
353 Airport Road
Oceanside, California 92054

760-722-7777
www.skateboarding.com

Museums
Huntington Beach International
Skate and Surf Museum
411 Olive Street
Huntington Beach, California
714-960-3483

Skatelab
4226 Valley Fair
Simi Valley, California
805-578-0040
www.skatelab.com

Skatopia
34961 Hutton Road
Rutland, Ohio 45775
740-742-1110

**Organizations, movers,
shakers . . .**
Action Sports Retailer
Organizer of the Action Sports
Retailer Trade Expos
949-376-8144
www.asrbiz.com

California Amateur Skateboard
League (CASL) and PSL
Amateur and professional
contest organizer
909-883-6176
Fax 909-883-8036

The Canadian Cup
416-960-2222

Extreme Downhill International
1666 Garnet Avenue #308

San Diego, California 92109
619-272-3095

International Association of
Skateboard Companies (IASC)
PO Box 37
Santa Barbara, California 93116
805-683-5676
Fax 805-967-7537
iascsk8@aol.com
www.skateboardiasc.org

International Network
for Flatland Freestyle
Skateboarding
Abbedissavagen 15
746 95 Balsta, Sweden

KC Projects
Canadian amateur contest
organizer
514-806-7838
kc_projects@aol.com
5148067838@fido.ca

National Amateur Skateboard
Championships
Damn Am Series
National amateur contest
organizer
813-621-6793
www.skateparkoftampa.com
www.nascseries.com

National Skateboarders
Association of Australia (NSAA)
Amateur and professional
contest organizers
61-2-9878-3876
www.skateboard.asn.au

The Next Cup
Southern California amateur
contest organizer
858-874-4970 ext. 114 or 129
www.thenextcup.com

Real Amateur Skateboarding
Amateur contest organizer
619-501-1341
realamateurskateboarding
@hotmail.com

Skateboarding Association of
America
Amateur contest organizer
727-523-0875
www.skateboardassn.org

Skatepark Association of the
USA (SPAUSA)
Resource for skatepark
planning/operating
310-823-9228
www.spausa.org

Southwest Sizzler
Southwestern amateur contest
organizer
918-638-6492

Surf Expo
East Coast trade show
800-947-SURF
www.surfexpo.com

United Skateboarding
Association (USA)
Skate event organizer
and action sport marketing/
promotions
732-432-5400

ext. 2168 and 2169
www.unitedskate.com

Vans Shoes
Organizer of the Triple Crown
skate events
562-565-8267
www.vans.com

World Cup Skateboarding
Organizer of some of skating's
largest events
530-888-0596
Fax 530-888-0296
danielle@wcsk8.com
www.wcsk8.com

Zeal Skateboarding Association
Southern California amateur
contest organizer
909-265-3420
www.zealsk8.com

Public skateparks / information about building and starting up

Consolidated Skateboards
(see *The Plan*)
www.consolidatedskateboard
.com

International Association of
Skateboard Companies (IASC)
PO Box 37
Santa Barbara, California 93116
805-683-5676
Fax 805-967-7537
iascsk8@aol.com
www.skateboardiasc.org

Skatepark Association of the
USA (SPAUSA)
310-823-9228
www.spausa.org

www.skatepark.org

**Public skatepark designers /
builders**
Airspeed Skateparks LLC
2006 Highway 101 #154
Florence, Oregon 97439
503-791-4674
airspeed@airspeedskateparks
.com
www.airspeedskateparks.com

CA Skateparks, Design/Build
and General Contracting
273 North Benson Avenue
Upland, California 91786
562-208-4646
www.skatedesign.com

Dreamland Skateparks,
Grindline Inc.
4056 23rd Avenue SW
Seattle, Washington 98106
206-933-7915
www.grindline.com

John Woodstock Designs
561-743-5963
johnwoodstock@msn.com
www.woodstockskateparks.com
Ramptech
www.ramptech.com

SITE Design Group, Inc.
414 South Mill Avenue,
Suite 210

Tempe, Arizona 85281
480-894-6797
Fax 480-894-6792
mm@sitedesigngroup.com
www.sitedesigngroup.com

Spectrum Skatepark
Creations, Ltd.
M/A 2856 Clifftop Lane,
Whistler, B.C.
V0N 1B2 Canada
250-238-0140
design@spectrum-sk8.com
www.spectrum-sk8.com

Team Pain
864 Gazelle Trail
Winter Springs, Florida 32708
407-695-8215
tim@teampain.com
www.teampain.com

**Shops /
finding one close to you**
Two (among quite a few) that
will help:
www.skateboarding.com
www.skateboards.org

**Skateparks /
finding one close to you**
Two (among quite a few) that
will help:
www.skateboarding.com
www.skateboards.org

**Television
ESPN**
X Games
espn.go.com/extreme

NBC
Gravity Games
www.gravitygames.com

Web sites
www.board-trac.com
Market researchers for skateboarding industry.

www.bigbrother.com
A comprehensive site by *Big Brother* magazine.

www.exploratorium.edu/skateboarding
Glossary, scientific explanations and equipment for skating.

www.interlog.com/~mbrooke/skategeezer.html
International Longboarder magazine.

www.ncdsa.com
Northern California Downhill Skateboarding Association.

www.skateboardiasc.org
International Association of Skateboard Companies (IASC) is one of the leading advocates of skateboarding progress and provides a wealth of information.

www.skateboard.com
Chat and messages.
www.skateboarding.com
Every skater's site by *Transworld Skateboarding* magazine.

www.skateboards.org
Find parks, shops and companies here.

www.skatelab.com
One of Los Angeles area's largest indoor parks and world's largest skateboard museum.

www.skater.net
Skate parks, ramp plans ...

www.smithgrind.com
Skate news wire

www.switchmagazine.com
Switch Skateboarding Magazine

www.thrashermagazine.com
A comprehensive site by *Thrasher* magazine.

More web sites
www.stevebadillo.com
vtaskate@aol.com
www.skatelab.com
www.bokasmo.com
www.tonyalva.com
www.pornstarclothing.com
www.dogtownskateboards.com
www.chocolateskateboards.com
www.dvsshoecompany.com
www.chapmanskateboards.com
www.teampain.com
www.rcmcsk8parks.com

Videos / Instructional

411 Video Productions. *The First Step.*

411 Video Productions. *The Next Step.*

Hawk, Tony. *Tony Hawk's Trick Tips Volume I: Skateboarding Basics.* 900 Films, 2001.

Hawk, Tony. *Tony Hawk's Trick Tips Volume II: Essentials of Street.* 900 Films, 2001.

Thrasher Magazine. *How to Skateboard.* San Francisco, California: High Speed Productions, Inc., 1995.

Thrasher Magazine. *How to Skateboard Better.* San Francisco, California: High Speed Productions, Inc., 1997.

Transworld Skateboarding. *Starting Point.* Oceanside, California, 1997.

Transworld Skateboarding. *Trick Tips with Wily Santos.* Oceanside, California, 1998.

Transworld Skateboarding. *Starting Point Number Two.* Oceanside, California, 1999.

More addresses

Alva Skateboards
403-B Wisconsin Ave.
Oceanside, California 92054

Bokasmo
2141-K El Camino Real
Oceanside, California 92054

Geometric Construction
2420 Industry Street
Suite C
Oceanside, California 92054
760-721-6798

SkateLab
4226 Valley Fair St.
Simi Valley, California 93063

Index

About the authors

Steve Badillo

Steve Badillo is a professional skateboarder and skating coach. He has skated on MTV and in numerous ads and videos including those of Limp Bizkit and Offspring. He coaches at Skatelab in Simi Valley, California and lives with his wife Becca and son Gavin in nearby Ventura. Steve's first skateboarding book, *Skateboarder's Start-Up*, was published in 2000.

Check him out at www.stevebadillo.com

Munns

Doug Werner

Doug Werner is the author of the internationally acclaimed *Start-Up Sports®* series. In previous lifetimes he graduated with a Fine Arts Degree from Cal State Long Beach, built an ad agency and founded a graphics firm. In 1994 he established Tracks Publishing. Doug lives with his wife Kathleen and daughter Joy in San Diego, California.

www.startupsports.com